Wisdom Comes Dancing

Wisdom Comes Dancing

Selected Writings of Ruth St. Denis on Dance, Spirituality, and the Body

Edited and with an Introduction by

Kamae A Miller

sm

PEACEWORKS
International Network for the Dances of Universal Peace
Seattle, WA

Introductory Essays, Notes, Appendices, and Edition
© 1997 Kamae A Miller

This book is printed in the United States on recycled, acid-free paper that meets the American National Standards Institute Z39.48 Standard.

Printing by Thompson-Shore, Inc., Dempster, Michigan

Book design by Anne Wysocki & Emily Smith, Houghton, MI, USA

CREDITS FOR PHOTOGRAPHY

Courtesy Dance Collection, The New York Public Library for the Performing Arts, Astor, Lenox, and Tilden Foundations: p.67, John Lindquist; pp. 68, 105, 112, Marcus Blechman; p. 101, Ricardo Amador; p.109, Soichi Sunami.

Courtesy Department of Special Collections, University Research Library, UCLA: pp. 61-64, 66-67, 69-70,102-103, 106-108, 110-111, photographers unknown.

Courtesy Sufi Islamia Ruhaniat Society (photograph a gift to Murshid Samuel Lewis from Ruth St. Denis): p. 104, Marcus Blechman.

Materials from the Ruth St. Denis Collection of the Department of Special Collections, University Research Library, UCLA, are reproduced with permission.

LIBRARY OF CONGRESS CATALOGING-IN-PUBLICATION DATA

St. Denis, Ruth, 1880-1968.
    Wisdom comes dancing : selected writings of Ruth St. Denis on dance, spirituality, and the body / edited and with an introduction by Kamae A Miller.
          p. cm.
    Includes bibliographical references.
    ISBN 0-915424-14-2
    1. Modern dance, Religious. 2. St. Denis, Ruth, 1880-1968. 3. Dance—Philosophy. I. Miller, Kamae A. II. Title.
GV1783.5.S7 1996
792.8—dc21   96-43529
                                                CIP

PEACEWORKS

International Network for the Dances of Universal Peace

444 NE Ravenna Blvd., Suite 306

Seattle, WA 98115-6467 USA

Editor's Note & Acknowledgments

Ruth St. Denis has been in my life a long time, not always consciously but hovering around since childhood. This project offered me a way to express my gratitude to a woman who was an artist, dancer, poet, mystic, and very human being. I am fortunate in requiring my heroes to have human qualities, thereby removing their need to be perfect.

I cannot remember when I first heard of Ruth St. Denis. It seems to me I always knew of her. She was often at a college in the village next to mine when I was growing up. I knew of her as a dancer. But in the early seventies a friend introduced me to her poetry. It moved me deeply. I recognized her not only as an inspiring dancer but as a mystic as well. About this same time I was initiated into the path of Sufism. I also acquired a copy of *An Unfinished Life,*

Ruth St. Denis' autobiography. The dense book was as beautifully written as the poetry and deepened my admiration for her even more.

A year later I moved to San Francisco to pursue my Sufi studies. When I entered the meditation room of the Mentorgarten, the former home of Samuel L. Lewis, I saw a large picture of Ruth St. Denis in her Kwan Yin pose. It was inscribed to Samuel L. Lewis. As I became more aware of the history of the Dances of Universal Peace, I discovered that Samuel Lewis considered Ruth St. Denis to be the "grandmother" of the Dances.

My first and foremost debt is, of course, to Ruth St. Denis herself. Her inspiration and determination, expressed so often in her writings, helped me to carry on.

We are all indebted to Murshid Samuel L. Lewis, mystic, teacher and founder of the Dances of Universal Peace for keeping the thread of sacred dance envisioned by Miss Ruth alive. He said she taught him "how to pick dances out of the heart of God."

The Dances of Universal Peace are in certain way a response to Miss Ruth's desire that everyone, no matter what age or ability, could have the opportunity to express their highest potential in dance, with no one person being the star and with no commercial concerns, the only measure of success being the opening of hearts to beauty and the sacredness of all.

Without the dedication of Samuel L. Lewis' students we would not have these Dances today. Great gratitude to all his students who carried on his work after his passing, especially Wali Ali Meyer, Moineddin Jablonski, Jessica Hall and Vasheest Davenport.

Wisdom comes dancing...

Continuing in their footsteps, Neil Douglas-Klotz, along with many talented and dedicated people, created PeaceWorks International Network for the Dances of Universal Peace. Today PeaceWorks continues to serve as a network to connect people world-wide in their desire to create peace through the arts. By supplying information, audio tapes, books and seminars, they are an invaluable resource.

Miss Ruth left her personal papers to the University of California at Los Angeles (UCLA). Without their preservation we would not have the material we do today. There are still many more boxes of writings waiting to be explored.

The Library of Performing Arts at Lincoln Center has manuscripts and reviews of Miss Ruth and more writings on Denishawn. Their organization and easy access makes it possible for anyone to read about Miss Ruth, as well as see videos and films.

My gratitude goes to Della Lou Swan, who from the beginning supported this project in innumerable ways. She, Tasnim Fernandez, and Eva Latifah Cristofalo de Hermila assisted me in searching through the few boxes we requested from UCLA. Hamida Sandy Susut did leg work at UCLA that helped simplify a daunting task.

Sara Morgan reawakened my interest in Miss Ruth by giving PeaceWorks a copy of the manuscript "The Divine Dance," which was entrusted to her by Murshid Samuel Lewis.

Many people typed the materials on to computer format. It was not an easy task. Their contribution cannot go unnoticed. To you all, great thanks!

Ruhama Velfort was the first to take on the daunting task of editing the editor. Such a brave and supportive soul. Ayesha Foot has just the right sort of love for the words and eye for error to make an invaluable proofreader.

Gratitude to Arifa Miller, who shared with me her deep and transformative experiences with Miss Ruth. To my dance teacher, Klarna Pinska, a former pupil and dancer with Miss Ruth, who had the courage to go on dancing.

Appreciation to Ruth Harwood who created the beautiful drawings in this book. They originally appeared in *Lotus Light*, Miss Ruth's only published book of poems. Miss Ruth wanted her to illustrate her book on Divine Dance. I consider it a tribute to her to offer a new audience her fine drawings.

Blessing and thanks to the many friends world-wide who became enthused and pushed, prayed and supported me through this process.

Great thanks and appreciation to the past and present staff and Board of Directors for PeaceWorks, whose interest and heartfelt support made this project possible; especially Connie Brobeck, whose tact and patience eased my task. Neil Douglas-Klotz's support with this project and all of my life is deeply appreciated.

Table of Contents

 *Photographs* 59

Introduction

Ruth St. Denis was an artist, dancer, poet, mystic as well as one of the founders of American modern dance. She was also a very complex person. During her active career, both as a solo dancer and co-founder of the Denishawn Dancers, her thoughts on dance were published extensively. Rising and falling out of favor in the dance world, she continued dancing, studying, reading and writing until her death in 1968.

Her life has been examined again and again even in recent times, but although she spent the last nearly thirty years of her life focusing her energies on sacred dance in America, very little of this work in written form has been available to the general public.

Here in her own words through talks, poetry, and essays, Miss Ruth expresses her philosophy of sacred dance, her belief in the role of women in peace-making, her innate love of the earth, and her ever-present connection to the divine. In it all her beauty and brilliance shine. Although the materials here range in time from the early part of the century down through the early sixties, they are still a call to those who can hear, to help us re-engage our delight in art, movement, nature and life itself.

Like any great artist or composer, Miss Ruth returns repeatedly to the several themes that inspired and moved her throughout her whole life: the sacredness of the body, the necessity to integrate the self and the need to emphasize beauty and life. Although she awakened to "physical love" later in life, Eros is present in many of her works and words. Today we could learn from her sensuality, which was such that critics wanting to condemn her for her open ways were overcome with the beauty, purity, and subtlety of its expression.

In editing I tried to leave the voice of Miss Ruth unhampered. Most of the editing was done to make her spoken word sensible in written form. I have, however, tried to make personal pronouns gender neutral. Miss Ruth believed in androgyny and recognized that the qualities of both sexes are necessary for individuals to achieve completion. I have left the tense in the present, because even though these words were spoken or written over 30 years ago, she is as contemporary now as she was then. Such is the way with prophets.

Miss Ruth bequeathed her writings and pictures to the University of California at Los Angeles (UCLA). She was a prolific writer and chronicler of her own life. There are over a hundred boxes bursting with papers and photographs.

The New York Library of Performing Arts has a stunning collection of dance writings, books, pictures and films. Here the Denishawn era is chronicled

along with many articles Miss Ruth had published during her long life. Both institutions are invaluable as sources for more information on Ruth St. Denis. The book includes pictures that have been gathered from both collections.

Section 1 is a manuscript of the previously unpublished "The Divine Dance," Miss Ruth's term for dance that links spirit with body. A preface from one of the boxes at UCLA, entitled "Preface for Dance Book," is included at the beginning of the book. Unfortunately no other pages were found with it. It is possible it was another preface for "The Divine Dance."

She wrote most of "The Divine Dance" in 1934 and used it as a text for her talks at Adelphi College and probably other places as well. The manuscript was in the possession of Samuel L. Lewis and came to PeaceWorks through his student, Sara Morgan. The book itself has seven parts:

Chapter 1 talks about Miss Ruth's philosophy of the dance and the spiritual background that she believes necessary to sacred dance.

Chapter 2 emphasizes the body as an instrument of the divine rather than a mechanism.

Chapter 3 delves more deeply into the development and practical application of the Divine Dance.

Chapter 4, after a delightful appreciation of nature, gives ways for the solo performer to participate in the Divine Dance and shows how a group can work together, as well as avoid the pitfalls of group work.

Chapter 5 talks about the use of dance in traditional worship. Miss Ruth was a pragmatist in many ways. She knew that the majority of the people to whom she spoke were Christians. Although she had always been a mystic, open to the truth of all spiritual paths, she wanted to help energize the dominant religious culture.

Chapter 6 describes how, by realizing and living fully our ideal, we can be the herald of a finer humanity.

In Chapter 7, Miss Ruth describes, in a beautiful poetic way, the "Dance of the Future."

Section 2 of this book contains a series of lectures on aspects of sacred dance, which we found in the collection at UCLA. The first lecture was given at Jacob's Pillow in 1949. The rest were given at Miss Ruth's Society of Spiritual Arts in New York during the month of March 1936.

Section 3 gives examples of Miss Ruth's poetry, written throughout her life. In 1932 she published a book of poems called *Lotus Light.* Like all mystical poetry, that of Miss Ruth is easy to criticize as romantic and idealistic. When one has undergone surrender to a spiritual path, however, the poems become illumined as one recognizes a fellow traveler. Most of these poems were gathered from UCLA.

In Section 4 I have placed a series of writings that fit in no particular category but which express other interests of Miss Ruth's. These include a proposal for a sacred dance pavilion at the 1939 World's Fair; various manifestos and credos on principles of sacred dance; and an update on her interests in 1960, a few years before her death, written as a last chapter to "The Divine Dance."

The appendices to this book include annotated selections from Miss Ruth's autobiography, *An Unfinished Life,* as well as a bibliography of her favorite books.

In reading Miss Ruth it is important to remember what Walter Terry says in *Miss Ruth: The "More Living Life" of Ruth St. Denis* (New York: Dodd, Mead & Co., 1969.):

> To understand *Miss Ruth* in either 1917 or 1967 and all the years before
> and in between, it is absolutely essential to accept the paradoxes which made
> her what she was.... She was reverent and irreverent in a matter of seconds,
> and the paradox should never have been subject to condescending forgiveness,
> for one was as much a part of her nature as the other. The androgyny—the
> recognition of the female element and the male element in all beings, and
> especially in artists—was echoed in many other manifestations, in kindness
> and cruelty, in humility and arrogance, and in discipline and disorder.

Wisdom comes dancing…

Short Biographical Essay

I will try to condense what was a long and fruitful life full of mountains and valleys, fame and obscurity, creativity and emptiness, love and loneliness. In the first appendix I have offered Miss Ruth's description of some of the highlights of her life until 1939 from her autobiography, *An Unfinished Life*. Throughout this book, I refer to Ruth St. Denis as Miss Ruth, as her many students and friends did throughout her long life. In this section, however, I have used whatever name she used during that particular period of her life.

Miss Ruth had three gods that called her to worship—religion, art, and love—and she was always in the process of trying to balance them. In her dance she sometimes achieved this precarious balance, but she found that in life this was not an easy task.

Ruthie Dennis was born on a farm in New Jersey, to a couple not particularly suited to each other. Her mother was an ambitious, strict Methodist medical doctor. Her father was a transcendentalist, dreamer, philosopher and inventor. Although she stopped practicing formal medicine, Ruth's mother was often the one who supported the family by taking in boarders. This situation did not seem to daunt Ruth, who probably used these people as her early audiences. Temperamentally she resembled her father, taking an interest in nearly everything but especially philosophy and, through that, religion. She read the Bible throughout her life, a practice she picked up from her mother. Paradoxes abounded in her life and those of her parents. Although a strict Methodist, Ruth's mother was the one who encouraged her dancing, paid for her movement lessons, supervised her practice sessions and became Ruth's manager as she began her stage career.

After a series of acrobatic performances as a young teenager, she gave up on movement temporarily and did a number of other jobs, including modeling in a department store and racing a bicycle for money. Finally, under the famous impresario David Belasco, she played some small parts on the stage. Because she was a vivacious and fun-loving girl who kept herself free from physical entanglements, Belasco "canonized" her Ruth St. Denis. During this time she also read *Science and Health,* by Mary Baker Eddy, which had a great influence on her philosophical approach to life. While on tour in Buffalo, New York, in 1904 with a Belasco production, she had an "ah ha" experience staring at a poster for Egyptian Deities cigarettes. Seeing the seated Isis, suddenly she knew what she was meant to do.

Upon returning to New York she told her family of her vision. They supported her in the desire to work on a dance that would embody the spirit of Egypt. As she worked on this vision, it became clear that this particular dance or pageant would be too costly to produce. This factor led her to work on solo dances with a particular concentration on India. To research this, she read *The Light of Asia,* scriptures from Hindu and Buddhist traditions and any other books she could find about India. This also marked the time when she became aware of her belief in the unity of various diverse religious ideals.

Performance dance at this time was pretty much limited to vaudeville or ballet. There was no such thing as modern dance—either artistic or sacred. The faith of her family and that of herself in her destiny must have been very strong to attempt to break the bounds of what was normally thought of as art or even popular entertainment.

Section 4 of this book contains a synopsis of the dance, *Radha, Delirium of the Senses,* written down in 1904 for copyright purposes. Even now it might stretch a few people's imaginations. This dance began a thread that Miss Ruth would follow in many dances, that of embodying a sacred female figure. I do not use the term embodying lightly. Miss Ruth would always meditate and create a sacred atmosphere before she danced. This atmosphere permeated her performances and often surprised her audiences, both in the theater and in the variety hall. She continued this practice her whole life and passed it on to her students as well.

Beginning with *Radha, Delirium of the Senses*, she created a cycle of East Indian-inspired dances. The cycle included *The Cobras, The Yogi,* and *Spirit of Incense. Radha* was presented first in January 1906. The others evolved shortly thereafter and most were presented through May 1906 in New York City. It was here that she achieved her first success.

As many artists did and still do to gain recognition, she immediately went to Europe after her New York run, at the advice of her agent, Henry B. Harris. Her initial reception in England and France was polite interest, but in Germany particularly she became a sensation. There many of the leading artists, poets and intellectuals sought her company. All the excitement and attention was heady stuff for this young woman, who was ever under her mother's watchful eye. Her mother tried to keep both Ruthie's and the young men's ardor under control. Here began an attraction that was to repeat itself throughout most of her life. The men most attractive to her were either homosexual or bisexual. For the most part they seemed to have a greater interest in the arts, poetry and metaphysical ideas that so interested her. They were also very handsome. One such liaison caused her mother so much distress she left Europe. Ruthie remained with her brother.

She spent two and a half years in Europe where she performed in variety halls but also in more elegant theaters like the Komische Opera in Berlin and La Scala in London. These were great years for Ruth as a solo dancer. The European audiences, being more open to other cultures, had more sophistication and seemed more able to appreciate and understand what she was trying to do. Ruth was twenty-eight when her dance career really began.

When she returned to the United States in 1909 as a star, her agent Henry B. Harris set up special matinee performances to reintroduce her to the New York public at the Hudson Theater. In a very daring move he also scheduled a series of evening performances in December of that year. No solo dancer had ever been presented as an evening attraction before. Ruth titled the offering "A Program of Hindoo Dances" including *The Cobras, The Yogi, The Nautch, Incense,* and *Mystic Dance of the Five Senses (Radha).*

Imagine at a time when women were still fully covered, when the norm was corsets and full-length skirts and when an ankle was a startling thing to see—a young woman, midriff showing, feet bare, dancing a dance of the senses. The expected reactions might range from outrage to titillation but early reviews found the audience often in stunned silence. The sacredness of

Wisdom comes dancing...

the atmosphere created was so great that it usually left people perplexed, as though they had been in a church or other holy place.

After the successes in New York, her agent sent Ruth on her first U.S. tour through the East Coast. Later a coast-to-coast tour was arranged. On one of the first of these, she was accompanied by the Khan family, one of India's most famous groups of musicians, who performed in some of her dances and often gave a short concert before she danced. One of the troupe who was actually on stage with her during her performance of *The Yogi*, was Pir-O Murshid Hazrat Inayat Khan, the great Sufi teacher. We can only speculate, but it is easy to imagine the conversations that might have occurred due to Miss Ruth's insatiable curiosity about spiritual subjects. This tour was significant in another way, for in one of the audiences was a young man who was to change Miss Ruth's career and life forever: Ted Shawn.

She toured the United States several times in the next four years as a solo performer. As an artist she worked very hard in her life to keep her vision clear and be honest with her dance. She often spoke of her three "gods"— art, religion, and love. As a solo performer she had much success; as a woman she had many flirtations and admirers but no real lover. She was now 32 years old. Her spiritual life was alive and well, but the god of love was demanding attention. As a woman she longed for human love. She also felt the pressure of dancing alone as a soloist for six years. She advertised for a male partner. She was ripe when Ted Shawn walked into the room. He was another of the beautiful boys—sensitive, charming and attractive to men. He also worshipped dance and, with it, Miss Ruth. The inevitable happened. They became dancing partners and lovers, but to preserve propriety they also were married a few months after meeting, much to the distress of Miss Ruth's mother.

If Ted had been only an acolyte to Miss Ruth's ideas, things might have been different, but he was ambitious and had his own ideas. Miss Ruth was never a good organizer, but she went along with many of Ted's ideas and therein lies the tale. They danced together and as soloists, but that was not enough for Ted. He felt they needed to pass on their technique to others, so they started a summer school. This did bring others, such as Martha Graham, Doris Humphrey and Charles Weidman. Soon there was a troupe, now named Denishawn.

The Denishawn Dancers toured for more than ten years, beginning in 1915. The band of players changed often. For most of the time, Louis Horst was musical director. From 1918 to 1920, Ted and Ruth worked on separate artistic visions but then returned to dance together as a duo and with the troupe.

While touring continued, Ted decided a permanent home must be found for the Denishawn ideal, Miss Ruth, and himself. In 1927, property was purchased in New York City and a beautiful building was erected as their home and studio. Miss Ruth's creative juices did not flow in such a structured environment. Poetry became even more a solace as the gap between Ted and herself widened. In 1932 a book of her poems, called *Lotus Light,* was published.

Miss Ruth's interest in metaphysics continued, however. Here she started talks and discussion groups, first named the Society for Spiritual Arts, and later renamed the Church of the Divine Dance. To these talks came many of the famous intellectuals, spiritual leaders and artists of the day, among them Nicholas Roerich, the Russian artist and metaphysician, and Rabindranath Tagore, the Indian poet and philosopher. These were compensations for Miss Ruth, but it was not enough. Ted moved out of the house in the early thirties

Wisdom comes dancing…

and began his own work with male dancers. He also began creating a center for dance, Jacob's Pillow, in northwest Massachusetts.

In 1934, the New York property went into receivership and Miss Ruth had to move. Friends rallied to her aid and she moved into a loft that was refurbished for her. She had sunk to a low point in her life. Her style of dance was rejected by the new dancers as old fashioned. In her view, dance had become mechanistic, angular, and ugly. She continued to write on the subject of sacred dance and put all her energy again into that which she knew was her purpose in life. The Thursday meetings of the Society for Spiritual Arts continued. From these meetings the Rhythmic Choir evolved, a group of dancers that would perform as part of a worship service.

Her next phase began: sacred dance became the main focus for the rest of her dance life. First she wished to bring dance into churches as part of the regular worship ritual. The next logical step was to start a Church of Divine Dance, where dance itself could be the main form of worship. This form of dance-ritual would be divided into different forms according to age and ability, but everyone would join in.

In 1938, when Miss Ruth was again impoverished, Paul Eddy, who had attended the Thursday night gatherings, invited her to start a dance department at Adelphi College on Long Island, where he was president. She designed the program and wrote and visited there well into the sixties. At about this time Miss Ruth got down to business and wrote her autobiography, *An Unfinished Life,* published first in 1939. The title proved prophetic, for she lived for another almost thirty years.

As all long lives go, Miss Ruth experienced many ups and downs, but for the most part she lived in the present. As her fame would be periodically revived and illuminated over the years, journalists would want to speak of her sparkling past. Miss Ruth would frustrate their attempts with, "Darling, this is what I am doing *now*." She had a remarkable ability to be honest with herself. She spent long hours of oberservation and self-reflection trying to understand herself and her actions. In her diaries she recorded these explorations. They offer a deep and instructive glimpse into the life of a woman who is both a timeless pioneer and prophet.

Wisdom comes dancing...

Section One

The Divine

Dance

Miss Ruth wrote the following manuscript on Divine Dance in 1934 while she was still living at the Denishawn house in New York. Life and the dance world seemed to be passing her by. Ted Shawn had left. The popular mode of movement was much more angular and mechanistic. Faced with all this, she redirected herself to her original vision and produced a definitive statement on sacred dance. In front of the body of the manuscript I have placed a preface we found at UCLA with no other related pages. It is a perfect introduction to her philosophy and spirit.

—KAM

Preface for Dance Book

All aboriginal people as well as every mature nation uses the dance as language, recreation, and entertainment. America should do more than repeat the past, taking what is good and leaving the rest. The American Dance of the future should rest upon a deeper understanding of life. Dance as an expression of that life should be more beautiful. Dance touches civilization at every point as art, health, business, amusement and morals. It is vital that it should be at once idealistic and practical.

This book is in no sense a history, a technical treatise or a summary of dance from an impersonal point of view. It is an intensely personal book dealing with dance as I see it and as my years of experience and growth have unfolded its meanings to me. I have tried to view dance, however, from that vantage point of human vision which does not subordinate the whole to the part.

I do not believe that to dance beautifully, or to be dedicated to the dance, will solve all our earthly problems or make us the dictators of health and wisdom. But as I believe that going upstream to the source of any one human activity leads us to our deeper selves, so do I believe that the dance holds within its vital elements the solution of many of our human problems, physical, emotional and spiritual.

My ideal of dance is that it should range itself alongside of the other arts in dignity and conception, in efficiency of technique and in service to the aims of a higher civilization.

To this end, our attitude towards the dance must change. We must cease to regard it as merely a conventionalized form of sex-expression, as the tired business person's amusement, or as an intellectual and geometrical problem unfolded to us at the concert hall.

Dance may be all these, but it is something more than these. Dance is a symbol of Life—rhythmic, glorious, immortal. It is a language and a hieroglyphic of divinity. Let us learn to speak it and to read it.

My personal attitude is that dance should have something to say, that its least message should be of life, not of death—of beauty, not of degradation. The geometrical and motional beauty that it gives the world should be a sign and manifestation of divinity. We have come upon evil days when our highest ideal of the dance is to make our bodies into dehumanized machines, or to watch five-year-old children strut around dressed up like Hollywood starlets.

The processes of this dedication are always the same: humility in learning inward wisdom, self-sacrifice and the discipline that will make us fit to reveal in terms of time and space the wisdom we have received.

In our present style, with only rare exceptions, we have neither temple nor acolyte. Our temple is a marketplace, and our acolyte to beauty is a salesperson. The fault for this lies, for the most part, in our immaturity towards the whole of Art and its necessary processes. Particularly in America today, the commercialization of Art is like the tail of a serpent over the whole of the land. We have an insane idea that everything must be sold. Our valuations of beauty or any gesture of it, are controlled by the amount that can be earned by it.

Until we learn in terms of experience instead of profits, we shall have neither a beautiful art of the dance nor a finer civilization.

Today we are asked to move our bodies to imitate the rhythms and motions of an artificial mechanism. We listen to the sounds of a staccato rivet and are asked to dance to that noise by way of expressing the modern mode. That may be the current rage, but why do it if it degrades the human body itself and lowers our concept of human dignity and beauty? We can do it, but why do it? What possible point is there in using the human body to reiterate the rhythms and motions of machinery? Why force the human body into the motions of a flywheel, or the thrust of a piston rod?

The human body is a machine, yes; the most perfect machine in the world, but it is more than that. The machine is an instrument, a tool, but the body is not only an instrument by which to express Life, it is a symbol of Life. It stands for human dignity and beauty, for intelligence and spiritual illumination.

The body is the receptive and the soul is the positive. If we are concerned with the mere mechanics and technique of what the body can be made to do, we lose the whole purpose and supreme value of the dance. As a rule, in proportion to our having nothing to say, do we invent extraordinary ways of saying it.

Either the young artist copies the externals of a new mode given by the choreographer without in the least understanding the reason and impulse of that mode; or the decadent artist, having no inspiration or fresh vision of life, concentrates upon the technique of an already full-grown expression. My quarrel with the young artists of today is that they are content to reflect the mechanical brutalities of a machine age whose instruments are largely those of greed and war. The minute that we analyze any art to its source, we come to the seat of motivations, the place of beginnings. We come to the quality of the individuals and their concept of Life itself. The body is a neutral instrument which reflects the minutest fraction of the consciousness that governs it. Every gesture reveals the level of consciousness that we have attained. It reflects in its rhythms and forms of motion either realization of Life vibrant, full of ecstasy, beauty, and continuity, or it reflects our negative states of fear, hatred, resentment, and false egotism.

In a word, have we not all of us a deep seated ideal of art, that it should be related to divinity.

The real message of the Dance is to open up the vistas of life to all who have the urge to express beauty, with no other instrument than their own bodies, with no apparatus and no dependence upon anything but space.... The Dance is at once the most satisfying and the most beautiful human activity.

Our Dance is the living sculpture of ourselves.

Wisdom comes dancing...

CHAPTER ONE

Spiritual Understanding and Realization

Our study should begin with what we are able to understand of the highest realization of truth that has been given to the world. We all need to be conscious of the eternal rhythm of life, that rhythm of spirit through which we may learn to move harmoniously and beautifully. I believe this rhythm is to be known and felt only as we spiritualize our thinking.

We must begin from the top and not from the bottom, from spirit, not matter, from God, not humanity. We must learn to withdraw the searching antennae of the mind from the circumference of outward activity to the inner and upper place of spiritual consciousness. From that level we may begin to realize our harmonious relationship with the causal rhythm of the universe.

By accepting a spiritual principle as our foundation we are at once started in an opposite direction from those forms and rhythms that have evolved from the physical basis of the heartbeat. As long as we accept the physical body as seen from the spatial world as our basis of action, we will continue to go over old ground, rhythms and traditions.

I do not believe that in the realm of the dance, going back to so-called primitive rhythms or learning to obey the rhythmic impulse of aboriginal peoples or children, will lead us to perfect freedom.

If we wish to unfold a new and more perfect dance which will be the rhythmic expression of spiritual consciousness, we must work from an entirely different viewpoint. Beginning with the principle of humans as spiritual beings, our first action is complete withdrawal of all activity on the former basis. Then the use of our body will become a thing of a new order. Spirit is felt as substance and body as a shadow.

Our conception of ourselves as born and dying, as physical and material, has inevitably produced certain activities of the body and certain forms of art. We have the material and beautiful rhythms of childhood, the athletic and stimulating dances of youth, and the toned gestures of maturity, but all are based on the accepted physical three-dimensional view of life.

Such spiritual realization as I have attained has come largely, though not entirely, from the study of the Science of Being as revealed by Mary Baker Eddy. I accept her statement of the real and spiritual identity of humanity, and I wish to found a system of dance, or rhythmical bodily culture, on this principle. I believe that my natural gifts and tendencies of study and aspiration have fitted me to pursue this line of unfoldment. The exigencies of a public career have often disturbed and suppressed my natural urge towards the atmosphere of spiritual radiation. But now I am happy at last to devote

my energies to the research and practice of a phase of the dance which has not, to my knowledge, been developed before.

My studies in Hindu and Buddhist literature gave rise to my first temple dance, *Radha*, which I felt at the same time to be a first gesture toward a new use of the dance as a means of spiritual expression. Since that time I have followed the path of a professional career as an artist and co-founder of Denishawn, but my deep interest in spiritual matters has never ceased. I feel that my third cycle of activity should deal with the consciousness of life as spiritual being and the expression of that realization in new and greater forms of beauty.

I want us to become conscious of being the inheritors of all truth, of all beauty, both from the past and into the unimagined future. I want to translate as far as I am able, this revealed truth into terms of beauty that shall open up new paths for the dance to follow, and bring new wonders for the soul to experience.

As an instrument of human living, the body is used for all the minutiae of our daily activities. When our center of attention has been changed from the response of the senses to external stimuli to the consciousness of spiritual being, we shall at once begin to breathe and move in a different manner.

The more we are involved in time and space activities the less we are able to reflect the infinite life. If the consciousness is solely concerned with reacting to this world of limitations, it will move in one way. If it seeks the realization of life, as spiritual, immortal, and perfect, it will move in quite a different manner.

A person's being is complete now, reflecting the masculine and feminine qualities which are truth and love. These qualities, however, must be expressed through the limitations of our time and space instruments.

I do believe that correct breathing and greater physical poise, strength, flexibility and grace will gradually accrue in the students' organisms, and will inevitably make itself felt in their whole lives. It will be apparent even in the least noticeable gesture of their existence. In a word, their daily life will reap the benefit of their scientific study of consciousness and its reflection in the body.

Observation is a part of our study, a valuable phase of our research. To know what other schools and individual artists are doing is good. We must interpret what we find, and in order to interpret constructively, we must have a living principle by which to gauge our standard.

A return to primitive drum-beats, primitive rhythms and movements, however minutely observed, however excellently transmuted into modern forms, is not advancing the experience of ourselves to higher levels of consciousness. Our true primitive and ultimate source is spiritual, and only as we rise to this consciousness in humility and truth can we begin to unfold greater and new life-releasing gestures of the body and discover new continents of beauty. Our real starting point is in inward acts of spiritual realization. It is not in observed gestures and rhythms of the body and it is not in response to audible stimuli, primitive, simple and seemingly fundamental.

We begin our lessons by conscious communion with the Invisible. From this state of communion we become aware of ourselves as instruments of the divine will which ever unfolds itself in beauty.

Wisdom comes dancing…

CHAPTER TWO

The Body as an Instrument of Spiritual Being

The time will come when our pride of life will return from the outward machinery and objects of our creating to the simple divine fact that resident within our own bodies is the greatest possibility of happiness and power. Instead of seeking to control external machines, we shall control ourselves in freedom and beauty.

For a long time we have lived constantly in two worlds, or we supposed we did, in body and in spirit. But the new waves of vision that have come over the earth have shown us that in reality there are not two warring substances but only one, which is consciousness or mind.

This being the case, our attitudes toward our bodies change, or should change. We should reverse our conception. We should realize in a vivid and revolutionary sense that we are not in our bodies but our bodies are in us. We create and control them, we use them to the ends of health and joy and vision.

Humans are related to the earth and to the heavens. We walk on the ground with our heads in the air. We eat of the food of the earth and are bathed in the sun's rays. We absorb every instant of our life, through breath and food, the elements which keep us alive. In turn, we give out in our work and play, through the body, the focused ideas and emotions that arise in us.

Our conceptions of the body vary, not only among different people, but in the same person from year to year. At one moment our conception includes an utter forgetfulness of the body in moments of extreme preoccupation. We think, feel and move without consciousness of the body. We are living in it and using it, but for the moment, in our conscious mind, it has no place. In the highest moments of emotional and artistic fervor, we are in a large measure unconscious of this instrument.

This however presupposes that the mood we are in does not require the use of the body beyond a nominal exertion and that the body itself is in a harmonious condition; that is, without conscious distress or pain. We were obviously meant to use our bodies and not to be conscious of them any more than the animals.

In our present mode of existence, however there are so many destructive and distorting forces of habit and condition playing upon us constantly that we are only too conscious of our bodily limitations and discomforts. It is to offset this fact that I am teaching the value of bodily training and use of the dance as the only ultimate, harmless and efficient way to correct many of our human ills.

To dance is to relate one's self to the whole of the Universe. By placing one's body in the direct power of rhythm it becomes molded and developed in strength and beauty.

There should be no period or age when the normal human body cannot be made in some measure pliable to rhythm. Good posture and movement are natural and beautiful. In this culture of a future race we should learn to walk like gods instead of shuffling and stumbling like mortals.

Our bodies are at once the receiving and transmitting stations for Life itself. It is the highest wisdom to recognize this fact and train our bodies to render them sensitive and responsive to nature, art and religion.

We should be like artists. Musicians regard their violin or piano with pride and care as the one thing necessary for their self-expression. Our bodies, likewise, should become the objects of our greatest concern. As musicians, once having tuned their instrument to the correct pitch, promptly forget it in the joy of its use and the beauty it reveals, likewise our bodies, having been trained and harmonized, will be forgotten in the joy of our use. At present we neither value our bodies nor know how to use them to get the maximum of joy and health that is possible.

In the case of the musical instrument there are whole industries devoted to the creating and manufacturing of perfect musical instruments for musicians to play. A fine musical instrumental is a precious and costly thing, yet those that can afford them love them for the beauty they make possible, and count them precious above all other objects.

We are playing upon these instruments of Life that are given us at birth, but surely we are clumsy players and neglectful guardians. We own the most marvelous machines in the world, yet I think we value a typewriter more than our own torso. We value a radio more than our own voices, and a car above our own legs.

How absurd it is when you think of it. We have the capacity to receive the messages of the stars and the songs of the night winds. We can hear the silent voice of the spiritual universe within our own hearts. We can scale the heights of the mountains and see the world rayed out below us, but we are like the blind calling loudly for color to be created or the deaf saying that someone should create sound.

It is all a question of valuation and what we believe will afford us the greatest measure of happiness. Perhaps all our action comes down to this: why do we do one thing rather than another, why do we abandon one experience for another unless it is that we hope the new experience will harmonize more nearly with our desires?

My conception of the Divine Dance of humanity is that through its medium we shall attain a finer, purer human experience than by any other method of joy or pleasure. The dance is innocent of error, is individual and independent in its expression and progress. The dance has no after effects of regret and harm. It calls out the best of intention and invention in its exponents and never leaves you where it finds you. You are always healthier and more alert in your mentality afterward.

It needs no expensive apparatus, is independent, and can be performed alone or in groups. It is economical to a degree when the commercial elements of corruption are renounced and people learn to dance without hope of gain.

Wisdom comes dancing…

Indeed it is this professional or commercial attitude toward the dance that is keeping it from becoming the universal and healthful recreation that it would normally be.

We should be content to experience and not compare, and to enjoy rather than to make money from this true gift of the gods.

When we look at a woman's or a man's body what are we seeing? Is it the real person we are looking at? Is this the real and ultimate body we are seeing, this fleshly and ponderous outline, or are we seeing a perfect instrument through the haze and distortion of our own limited and material viewpoint?

Does this body represent the soul or does it misrepresent it? The answer to these inquiries is that if we are to achieve a new and nobler dance through the instrumentation of a finer medium we must at the very outset abandon our old distorted conception of the body itself. With a totally new viewpoint of being and its instrument, we begin to work out the designs and patterns of a divine rhythm.

From a human viewpoint we shall always be dealing with this body of flesh and bones, of age and variation, of health and beauty, but from the spiritual understanding our whole approach will be at a different angle. We will have a realization of the power and joy that are inherent in the perfect instrument fashioned of the One Mind and existing now outside of the limitations of time and space.

Our body is an idea of the One Mind. It is now perfect, indestructible and immortal, but at present we can no more see it as it really is than can a person see clearly the objects in a darkened room. The whole trend of this inquiry is to attain gradually some glimpse of the divine instruments of ourselves and to reach some understanding of the immense possibilities of beauty, joy and power that these bodies contain.

To achieve this, however, we must do away with the traditional duality that has in the past so beset our theology. We must realize that the universe is one substance and that substance is spirit. The ultimate body, or instrument that we are dealing with is made of spiritual substance and is an idea of the Creating Principle of Life.

We are not made of one substance and our bodies of another. The whole scheme of things in reality is not two, but One. On this hangs not only the whole law and the prophets of the liberating philosophy of the new age but the very starting point and method of approach of the Divine Dance.

We are now the "children of God," and in the exact measure of our understanding of this spiritual fact will our interpretation of the human body and all its movements assume a different picture to our minds and deeper assurance to our hearts. We shall see that we are looking at the total person! We are looking at a child of God, a ray of the Divine Light, an idea of the One Mind.

This body is the articulation of the good, the true and the beautiful. Each member of its organism is the direct manifestation of Life. Each small gesture of its movement is the out-raying in time of the constant unfolding of Mind as reflected by the human soul. Nothing is unimportant, nothing is without meaning. Therefore our approach to the body as an instrument of life and art must be exactly opposite to the general conception.

At this point it will be of interest to recall the research of François Delsarte into the relationship of thought to movement, of emotion to motion.

François Delsarte was originally a French opera singer. He lost his singing voice and then decided to become an actor. He visited many of the schools of acting in Paris and found to his discouragement that each taught a different method. Each school disagreed with all the others and obviously had no universal principle upon which to build.

He then set out on a long period of research to discover the fundamental relationship which exists between thought and bodily motion. He did not come to America but a number of American students studied with him in Paris and brought back his influence to this country.

Among these students I know of three interesting personalities. Steele Mackaye became, perhaps, his greatest disciple. Mrs. Genevieve Stebbins also studied with him and had a small school of expression founded on his work.

When a child of eleven, I was taken to see Mrs. Stebbins in an unforgettable performance of Greek dancing. My whole artistic life was born at that hour. Therefore, I have always felt a deep debt of gratitude for the influence of Delsarte.

The value of Delsarte's research to the world of the dance lay in his discoveries regarding the relationship of the body as an instrument of emotional expression rather than in the rhythmic field of the dance.

His system includes the dividing of the body into three zones, the physical, the emotional and the mental.

The physical zone from the feet to the hips express the physical impulses of generation, work, play and all other space-covering activities.

The emotional zone between the hips and the shoulders, which contains the vital organs of heart and lungs, reflects the moods and intensities of our emotional life.

The mental zone of the shoulders and head represent the realm where thought is emphasized.

He found that all human expression, from infancy through old age, was based upon certain inevitable laws which govern the relation between consciousness and the zones of the body.

He recognized also the basic law of response: that all darkened consciousness, such as fear, sorrow and despair, is revealed in inward and downward movement, and that all joyous, affirmative thought is expressed in upward and outward movement.

This brief summary does not attempt to plumb the philosophic intent of Delsarte's teachings but only to draw the student's attention to the value of his discoveries relating to the body as a mobile instrument of expression.

In the broader interpretation of the body as a medium of expression it is first necessary to understand its natural reaction to mortal thought before we can regard it as a means of expressing Divine consciousness. Delsarte did not go into analysis of thought as to whether its source was mortal or divine.

Wisdom comes dancing...

CHAPTER THREE

The Divine Dance

The Divine Dance is the rhythm of spiritual affirmation! This dancing is called divine because it is our intention through posture, rhythm and progression to symbolize and manifest our spiritual realization.

In the dance, so far as I know, there has been no effort to define a line of demarcation between that movement that expresses erroneous consciousness and that which reflects the divine harmony.

The Divine Dance is that movement which symbolizes perfection, reveals immortal being and unfolds the dignity and meaning of humanity.

As we drop all errors of consciousness we shall also drop errors of movement. A new innocence will replace the artificial strain and self-consciousness of the dance artist who seeks to amuse, thrill and astonish. We shall wish to do none of these things but rather to experience the beauty of serenity and power. We shall heal and bless rather than astonish.

In the Divine Dance both the motivation and the instrument become purified, strengthened and beautified. This happens not merely through physical training but through the destruction in consciousness of those errors of belief which have limited and distorted this temple of the living God.

The Divine Dance is not merely dancing in a church or moving to religious rhythms. It is not the sublimating of mortal rhythms and meanings into finer forms of art.

The difference between secular and religious dancing is the difference between any other pair of opposites, particularly between a material and spiritual viewpoint of life.

If our dance is motivated by exhibitionism, personal pride, vanity, morbidity, envy, fear, or is used for erroneous propaganda we shall obviously see reflected in movement an overstrain, distortion and lack of dignity and balance. We shall know by the overtones of ugliness, futility and distress of mind that such dancing should be classed as secular.

My goal in this spiritually motivated art is to present to the world such noble and inspiring forms of the dance that all youth shall praise that principle which gave rise to such beauty. And maturity shall find such fresh joy of grace and strength that their faith in the ministry of beauty shall be renewed.

The supreme function of the Divine Dance is to quicken into activity the latent powers of truth and beauty in those devotees who are waiting for its kindling touch.

In this Dance of Divinity we become instruments of expression for that inner radiation of wisdom which is both our true life and our true art. The language of this dance is simple and direct and effortless, suggesting a translucence of body and movement for the luminous soul to shine through.

Even in our most perfect presentation of the Divine Dance, it must be remembered that its greatest value lies not in its excellence of rhythm and form but in its significance as a symbol of spiritual reality.

There is but one divine drama, the ritual of humanity's perpetual struggle toward liberation. The human drama of the Divine Dance is divided into three acts. In the first act we are putting into art form those aspirations and struggles of the human spirit which attend the accomplishing of any goal, be it artistic, scientific or spiritual.

First, there is the standing afar off, beholding the vision of beauty and power that the soul needs. This small flame within us is of the spirit itself and bears witness to the answering eternal flame. Before the first steps of our ascent begin there is the inevitable stage of discouragement and rebellion against the new discipline which seems to impose itself between us and our goal.

Our second act is the long period of discipline which all devotees must endure before they can control those elements of their own nature that constitute their bondage. This act expresses the receiving of the fundamental laws of work from their teacher and the practice and progression towards the mastery of their medium. In this final scene of ascent the climbers have attained sovereignty over their instrument and come to the realization of their spiritual identity.

The third and final act of our human drama begins at this point of realization. The fruition of this union with the divine is what we term radiation. Our radiation as artists gives forth of this light through the various time and space lenses of beauty.

As the sun fulfills its purpose of being by shining and only incidentally blesses the earth with its warmth and light, so is our life in spirit fulfilled with its own radiation of beauty and only incidentally affects and inspires its beholders.

It is the function of the divine artist in the temple to radiate in terms of beauty. Thus our ministry is primarily an experience of joy and only secondarily brings its inevitable results of healing and regeneration.

 *Practical Application*

Act I: *Vision and Discipline*

1. The student enters the classroom and is shown the Vision. The student resolves to become one with the Vision.

2. The student comes to the feet of the teacher and is given the first discipline.

3. The student becomes discouraged and rebellious and starts to retreat.

4. The student is now in a period of great bewilderment and mental suffering and only after great struggle comes to...

5. The point of surrender. Here the student lies prone upon the floor in an abandonment of surrender. This is the heart's offering upon the altar.

6. The last scene of our drama of discipline reveals the mental receptivity of the student who now sits quietly in an attitude of expectancy and enters into the great Silence.

Act II: *From Silence to Unity*

1. The response of body to the Divine Will begins with breath and the gestures growing out of this communion.

2. Rising—there are many ways of rising from the floor to standing position where the full articulation of the body is used. The simplest manner of rising will first be done, but as the student progresses more beautiful and controlled ways of rising will be attained.

3. Response—of the whole body to various forms of rhythmic discipline, which is symbolic of the discipline of the acolyte on all planes of being.

4. Covering space—taking all forms of walking, running, leaping and turning, circumference activities.

5. Conscious control—of the entire body, perfect coordination which includes examples of complete dance phrases.

6. Spontaneity and improvisation—The instant response to thought and music, expressed in coordinated movement.

7. Mystical union—between the realization of spiritual being and sovereignty over the body.

Act III: *Radiation*

Filled with the dynamic energy of spirit we ray forth our countless manifestations of beauty. These expressions range from the solo dance to the greatest complexity of large ensembles. This includes the improvised solo dances of offering in which the disciple moves in silent response to an inner mood, or in reaction to inspiring music, or poetry or scriptural passages. Among the forms of ensemble dancing are the interpretation of hymns, the antiphonal response to the center solo or duet figures, and the intricate patterns of an entire sacred ballet.

No one person or school can invent a whole new dictionary of human movement but can only add their small contribution to the whole glorious language of the dance. So we should with intelligent reverence draw from those rich funds of inspiration that are our inheritance from the past.

In the highest radiation of our present manifestation we shall utilize the full palette of colors composed of the finest contributions of the cultures of the world.

Our Temple shall be called the House of Praise!

Here the rhythmic beauty of the dance; the surge and wonder of music; the still yet vibrant forms of sculpture and painting; the mobile articulation of light beyond anything we yet have dreamed will all culminate in one grand orchestra with which to play our divine symphony of praise!

"For, behold, I create new heavens and a new earth... But be ye glad and rejoice forever in that which I create: for, behold, I create Jerusalem a rejoicing, and her people a joy" (Isaiah 65:17-18).

Wisdom comes dancing...

CHAPTER FOUR

Performance of the Divine Dance

After waxing eloquent about Nature, Miss Ruth gives guidance about the nature of solo and group dance from the point of view of the Divine Dance. —KAM

I. Communion with Nature

I remember once in Estes Park, Colorado, I was camping with my brother and his wife beside one of those beautiful little lakes that seem to lie motionless in the cup of the mountains. It was twilight and a strange light illumined the grandeur of the scene. Beside the lake there was a great rock shaped like some primitive altar which called one to a mood of outpouring praise for so much beauty. I ran around the still, blue lake and up the rocky steps of this natural altar and standing on the topmost ledge I sang a hymn of praise to the stars and the majesty of the mountains and the great Spirit of Creation pervading the valley.

In harmony with the subtle movement of the stars I also moved. I felt myself dancing with the earth because I was carried in its rhythmic turning, and an inward rhythm of great strength and calm filled my entire being.

It was for me one of those high moments of vision! I felt that such a valley was like a chalice held in God's hand, and here should come all nations and all races in a spirit of peace to revere and to hear the voice of the Eternal Song breathed into the pure serenity of the sky.

There are a thousand rhythms with which we are unacquainted as yet which would give us innocent and beautiful joys.

The rhythm of the sea! The feel of the wind and sun! The wild joy of the breakers! How instinctively we shed everything we can when we arrive at the ocean's edge! We run and leap and shout and whirl and finally fall exhausted upon the cool sands, full of a delicious fatigue. Tired and yet happy! The blessed sea has given us its ecstasy.

Or on a mountain top, in the calm of evening, with the eternal stars shining in splendor over our heads, how naturally we lift our arms in adoration. Our feet scarcely move, but our arms and hands are raised in a strange longing to attain the wonder and solemn beauty of the night.

Or on the plains, or on a smooth velvety lawn, who has not yearned to kick off their shoes and tread the soft moist earth in springy steps of sheer pleasure!

Oh, how much Nature has to give! How glorious and free and unending are the joys God has already provided for our health and happiness, and how we neglect them and make for ourselves surroundings of unrighteousness and death.

We sever ourselves from the inward inspiration of the Divine Breath and from the free, life-giving currents of Nature. Within the confines of our minds we create an entirely artificial universe where we finally suffocate and die.

Two of the world's most artistic nations have been first great nature lovers, and secondly, great creative artists. The Greeks, in their beautiful bodily contacts with the elements, have evolved for us the most perfect ideal of the heroic human body.

The Japanese have been nature lovers more from a mental and aesthetic sense and have therefore developed the art of painting in which the human body is portrayed in a beauty subservient to the harmony of the scene.

The art of this continent should seek to blend the attitudes of both these great cultures.

How small a unit we seem to be in the great whole when we regard ourselves as in opposition to Nature or independent of God! Yet, instantaneously we become expanded to unbelievable dimensions when we acknowledge our relationship to our spiritual source and our sympathetic contact with the infinite wealth of Nature.

II. *Solo Dance*

Now with these brief examples of Nature's lavish gifts in mind, let us turn to the subject of the solo dance on all its planes. As an approach to this let us ask ourselves these questions: Are there any instinctive differences in our dancing alone and dancing to be seen? What are our motives for dancing? Do we like to be watched or do we dislike it? Do we dance mostly in our minds or in our bodies? Do we take greater pleasure in planning our dances or in actually doing them?

Do we find it difficult to get the right conditions for dancing, either in natural or human-built settings? Does the average dancing school studio inspire us to dance? If not, what place, what architecture, what music, what lighting, what costume does inspire us?

How often we have said, "Oh, how I wish I could have a large and beautiful space to dance in, with all the music I want and lovely costumes and a mirror!" But there it has generally ended. Has it never occurred to us that by cooperation something might be done to give many of those of like interest a chance to express themselves.

There can be two major motives for the solo dance. One is the self-expression phase or desire for exhibition which is normal to the artistic temperament. The other is the purely sensuous delight in bodily motion which may be felt also in swimming, walking, or any other rhythmic exercises of a non-competitive character.

The solo dancer's artistic and professional career has a certain procedure of its own which cannot be dealt with here. This approach concerns the solo dance as an emotional release or as an expression of divine adoration.

Wisdom comes dancing…

Though the motivations of the two approaches are different from the outset, much of the basic training at the beginning may be the same, for the amateur as well as the professional should have a well-controlled bodily instrument.

The one way leads to the finished product of artistic creation and the other to self-realization through the path of rhythmic beauty. The fundamental difference between the two is that in the first training there is little or no necessity for any spiritual understanding while in the second the outward growth is dependent upon the inward spiritual realization.

I am now speaking largely of the amateur, presumably in the beginning stages of the dance as an expression of sacred ritual. Yet as I am a professional myself, I realize that here and there in the commercial world of the dance there are those individuals who are capable of deep spiritual understanding.

III. *Group Dance*

In all times people have danced together for the sheer joy of it. Social and religious dancing has brought people together in harmony through the unifying power of rhythm. Even the animals dance together for various purposes, both protective and joyful. We often find however, that we have not outgrown our childish delight in certain unthinking forms of artistic enjoyment, while in all other walks of life we have progressed with our years and are really adults in appreciation. This is particularly true of us Americans as a whole. Our business and scientific life is keen, mature and progressive, while our life of pleasure is almost infantile in its stupidity and repetitious character. As Yvette Guilbert [born in 1869, a French diseuse, known in her youth for songs in the Latin Quarter of Paris] so aptly says, "The childishness of Americans when they are taking their pleasure is the most fatiguing side of

American life." We have given very little wholesome constructive thinking to our amusements, leaving them to the imagination of Hollywood and Broadway, if not indeed to Coney Island [or Disneyland and Las Vegas].

Personally, I have lived to see many artistic epidemics sweep over the country. They come and go with a curious regularity in all phases of amusements. This is particularly true of the dance. For perfectly sound reasons the classic ballet has renewals of interest and manages to survive the fads. For its contribution of beauty and technical exactness to our development we are always thankful, but I believe that any thoughtful American dancer will agree with me that our ultimate dance form will not be the ballet.

We are on our way to something greater than the ballet! We are on our way to the greatest art of dance that the world has ever known. We are not only endowed with the physical requirements necessary for such an art but with a spiritual life that is vigorous and expanding. If we can correlate these elements of our individual and collective talents, we can enjoy the transcendent power and beauty of an art that is the result of self-control and self-realization, both professionally and in the field of recreation.

Those of us who study the dance as a direct language of spiritual expression should look carefully into the current fashions to find out what is of value in them. We may find often much that is not only delightful but sound in principle of beauty, but just as often we may find much that is merely the style of the hour, which is artificial and ugly.

I do not think it wise to make oneself conspicuous in ordinary social life by attempting other dances than those that are of the current fashion. At the same time there is also no reason at all for not seeking new and beautiful forms to raise the standard of enjoyment. The responsibility for this search lies, of course, with the creative dancers. Their offerings should be made so attractive that their beauty will inevitably permeate into the social realms. Group dancing naturally comes under two distinct schools, that of social and that of art dancing. We must consider them both in relation to our inner needs.

At the very outset we come to the question of our emotional constitution. How great a part shall it play in the motivations of our dancing? In this brief presentation of the subject it is impossible to go into it fully but we must grapple with the usually avoided issue of the relation of sex to art and the body. The moment that the spiritual dance is spoken of, the general mind at once conjures up the traditional ascetic mood in which the dancer is assumed to be quite sexless. This does not mean for a moment that the dancer is sexless but that we set up separation in our minds, dividing what we consider spiritual from that which is carnal and material.

My understanding of the whole matter rests upon two fundamental spiritual facts. First, that there is but one Substance. Second, that humanity is the reflection of a compound of the complete Principle which we term Love and Truth or our Mother and Father God. This Principle is our Creator, Sustainer and Governor. In our so-called physical state we find ourselves born into a body that is either masculine or feminine in its form, reaction and motivations. We also find to our great bewilderment that we are at times a strange blending of both of these elements; in a word, we find evidence of our complete Selves.

The whole subject of human movement can be approached only by obtaining a key or basic principle of line and rhythm from which to proceed. We have such a key, and only by the application of this principle can we arrive at any true judgment or enduring beauty. The first simple unalterable fact in our key is that the masculine line of truth is straight and the feminine line of love is curved. The love qualities are expressed in circular, fluid, space-covering rhythms while the truth elements are manifested in geometric and powerful forms of stability.

The flowing beauty of the sea has ever symbolized the feminine, while the mountains suggest the dignity of the masculine. In a spiritual sense each is ultimately the perfect Being, containing the two balanced forces of truth and love, but as soon as we begin the duet or group dancing we are dominated by one of these forces more than the other. Our dance then becomes the symbol of our struggle to attain the realization of our true and complete Selves. Philosophically speaking, we begin our study of the group dance by understanding ourselves as the spiritual reflection of the Mother-Father God. We analyze the gestures expressing that realization and the necessary discipline which must attend that activity.

A man and a woman dancing together in harmony of an exalted movement can become a symbol of the creative force of divine love.

We know that rhythm in itself is impersonal and universal, limited neither to individuals nor races. There are certain basic movements and rhythms which are normal to both sexes and should be practiced. There are countless patterns to be expressed by the group which cannot come into existence through the solo dance. There are emotional states which can arise only by harmonious cooperation of many in a unified idea. At the same time there has lately come into vogue such an accent upon the constant working together of the group that I wish to point out a few salient facts in relationship to this.

First of all, the inevitable tendency of the ensemble dance is to lessen the progress and responsibility of the individual dancer. The dancers grow more and more to look unthinkingly to the leadership of someone over them or to respond unresistingly to an idea which is given them. They begin to reflect in action whether or not they know anything of its meaning. Dictatorship in the dance is here seen to be the bad outcome of too much mass movement.

The artistic mind as a rule has considerable contempt for the average folk dance. One reason is that, like hymn singing and other forms of general cooperation, the form used has rarely progressed from that which is used by the majority. It is therefore very simple and has the tendency to circle about a very limited area of expression. Group dancing of the divine expression should be progressive. It should reveal in action the ceaseless expansion of Mind as it is reflected in the individual consciousness.

For individuals starting their first efforts in group work it is well for them to be aware of this involved principle. The instant they become part of a group their reaction must become feminine or receptive to the idea or person dominating the ensemble, although the work being done may be masculine and positive. Even in what might appear to be the greatest liberty of action there must be a unity of movement, or it cannot rightly be called group dancing. Though there is no place for personal initiative in many of the group activities there is a rich enjoyment in moving with one's fellows in patterns of rhythm and beauty.

There is the possibility of group work done in a more spontaneous manner in response to simple drum beats or more complicated musical themes. For instance, take a group of some twelve or fifteen dancers standing close together in the center of the studio. They are in a relaxed and attentive mood ready to respond to any stimulus. In group dancing for enjoyment, each individual should be a potential leader, capable of directing the movements of the group. This capacity should be encouraged by the teacher of the work. The leader strikes the chord and the entire troupe instantly responds, either in a unified pattern already suggested or with individual variations in keeping with the theme.

As we in this dance movement are primarily concerned with the dance as sacred, our group work begins with the question of leadership. Who or what is our master? The Divine Dance should reflect what is good, inspiring and beautiful of any age and race. To achieve the highest leadership it is obvious that we must lift our gaze from the confusions of humanity to the oneness of the Christ consciousness. Thus, the group of the Divine Dance becomes the symbol of the human unity held together by the dynamic rhythm of the manifested Cosmic Christ, spiritual truth.

CHAPTER FIVE

The Relation of the Divine Dance to Sacred Ritual

The age of preaching is slowly passing, and the age of expression is upon us, the age of revelation by all manner of new means of beauty.

Today we are at the beginning of a great renaissance of the dance. The Divine Dance is immortal. It can speak the message of spiritual power and beauty in terms of rhythm, tone and color better than any other means, for as Havelock Ellis says, "The Dance is not only the supreme manifestation of physical life, but the supreme symbol of spiritual life!" (*Dance of Life*. New York: Grosset, 1923, p. 34).

A number of years ago while playing in a small town in the South we had Sunday night free of travel, so a friend and I decided to go to church. We entered one of those typical red brick buildings that are found in every town and village. A small congregation straggled in, mostly those of elderly character. A few lights flickered dimly in the place, which was very drab, bare and devoid of any touch of vitality or beauty. The monotonous droning of the minister giving the sermon, the lugubrious hymns, all sung in the same somber key of resignation, completed the atmosphere of gloom.

After an interval of this we were glad to return once more to the beauty of the stars. We walked some blocks toward our hotel and, in turning a corner, we suddenly came upon a movie theater. It was ablaze with light, and the facade of the theater itself was colorful and attractive. Pouring forth from its doors was the well-dressed, laughing, chattering youth of the town.

A great resentment and a kind of righteous indignation welled up in my heart, and I was jealous for the church. Suddenly I had a vision of a great beautiful edifice with light and motion and harmony as its expression. It was a "Temple of the Living God." It has all the land, the beautiful and sublime architecture, the most attractive decorations and lighting and, above all, the most vital, beautiful men and women as its ministrants and congregation.

This vision of the House of God was alive, as irresistibly attractive to youth as to maturity. Jesus said, "I came that ye might have Life and that ye might have it more abundantly." Surely this Life means a living realization expressed in terms of highest Beauty.

If the consciousness of our union with God is not a joyous, living experience, surely it is not genuine. If it is such a joyous and exalting experience, we will want to express it through speech, writing and singing.

Wisdom comes dancing...

But why stop there? Can we not move our whole body in rhythmic movement that is harmonious and life-enhancing? Is there any reason why we should not dance? It is useless to say that the dance has been debased and is everywhere performed by immoral and sinful people. Speech has been put to the vilest use, song and all the other arts have been made at times to serve ignoble and futile ends. Because this is so we cannot dispense with all speech, song, line, or color to express the wonder and vitality of our spiritual realization.

I passionately want religion to have all the principalities and powers, not only the science of the intellect and the sacrifice of the heart. I also want the church in its highest non-sectarian sense—Christ's gospel of Life—to have the irresistible lure of beauty with which to heal and inspire the world.

In this transitional period of the Divine Dance, it is natural that we should use certain of the beautiful, older forms of ritual to introduce rhythm into all manner of religious services.

My concept of the new forms of worship that would include rhythmic movement in the church services asks for no lessening of the natural dignity and solemn beauty of spiritual realization. But I call for a new, vital expression that will bring humanity into a closer, more harmonious relationship with the One who created our bodies as well as our souls.

Looking into the future, I see thousands of churches pulsing with life and revealing the beauty of holiness; I see thousands of altars where the young Miriams and Davids of today are dancing before the One! I see maturity reborn in grace and strength, and the joyous footsteps of the children dancing down the chancels of the world, bringing to the shrine of God their offerings of praise!

CHAPTER SIX

The Herald of a Finer Humanity: Manifesting the Christ

If we could look into an X-ray large enough to take in the entire human figure and if we could see clearly the transparent wonders of this organism, we would obtain a new vision of ourselves. Even by holding up our hands in the strong sunlight until we see our fingers in a vivid glory we can grasp a faint idea of the beauty of the body.

What a great mystery it is and yet how casually we regard it!

When we are really persuaded that the human being itself is more worthy of our intelligent thought than any other object in the world, we shall unfold the infinite capacities of our inherent Divine Inheritance.

If we are not now the "joint heirs with Christ," when shall we be? The spiritual fact of our eternal inheritance comes to us in unbelievable, astounding power! We pause and wonder. We withdraw from the world of our hurrying days and enter the Sanctuary where we may let this meaning take full possession of our beings.

To manifest the Christ! How stunned we are at the very thought of it! How instantly we swerve away from any conception of embodying the Christ. The very web of our traditional feelings prevents the acceptance of the bodily glory and radiance of the Christ. As long as we insist upon dwelling in the valley of self-condemnation and fear, looking at a far-off Christ, so long shall we reap the bitter fruits of our duality.

How can we achieve perfection in practice if we do not assume it first in consciousness? To manifest It, we must first be It! Until every least need and thrill of the full octave of human experience finds fulfillment in the Self of the Christ we shall not abandon the mortal self with its world of illusions.

What would we do if we were manifesting the Christ? Would not the rhythm of our walk, the posture of our bodies, the gestures that we make in work and play be of a different order? And the thoughts that motivate our movements—would they not be from a higher source?

Manifesting the Christ would mean raying forth the power, beauty and joy of the Divine into the minutiae of every moment of our life. It would mean shedding the outworn forms of existence that have been generated by fear and lust. In our sleeping and waking, our loving and working we would be ever conscious of our infinite capacity for happiness and freedom.

Until we experience the mystic marriage of the soul with the Christ, until we experience the "Christ conquest" of the body in full identity and power, we cannot know the true meaning of the Divine Dance. In our old dispensation of "righteousness and peace" we made little provision for the dynamic, progressive and expressive unfoldment of our joy. As a symbol of the new spiritual dispensation the Divine Dance comes offering one of the greatest experiences of joy in the whole gamut of human potential.

From this viewpoint of life, we begin from the center with the purification of the first environment, our own garment of flesh, and by the conception of our bodies. From there we radiate outward into the surrounding world. In stillness we know, we feel, we realize. In silence we become aware of the divine river of our life flowing from an inner source. In silence we disconnect ourselves from the swirling atoms of discord and unfold ourselves in strength and beauty. In silence we perceive the Lotus of the Law, opening its petals in order, proportion and harmony. It is vibrant with life, perfect in design and luminous with love.

In the dream life in which we seem to live, we thrash about caught in the meshes of the world, in pain, loneliness, lust and fear. But in the place that is the truth of our existence, these discords and frustrations are not known.

For here we walk in spirit. We move in love and not in fear.

CHAPTER SEVEN

The Dance of the Future

The dance of the future will no longer be concerned with meaningless dexterities of the body but will move in harmony with the compassionate and joyous rhythms of love, and will obey in strength and balance the vital laws of truth. Here upon the eternal lotus pattern of love and truth the Divine Dance treads the measures of eternity in praise!

Sometimes we look downward and halt and stumble, losing for a time the vision of our birthright in the perfect pattern, but in reality we are always the immortal Being, born of love and truth. For "In the order of Science, in which Principle is above what it reflects, all is one grand concord." [Probably from Mary Baker Eddy.]

This glorious pattern of perfection becomes indeed the keynote of the arts of the future. To those who understand its language, each fragmentary gesture will reveal some quality of the whole. In the Divine Dance the two creative forces of love and truth have their own rich variations of beauty. In the dance of love we move in exquisite, flowing rhythms from the center of our being outward toward an infinite circumference. In the more austere gesture of truth, we have a sense of design and balance, basically formed from the pure geometric laws of the cosmos.

Remembering that a human being is indeed the microcosm, the universe in miniature, the Divine Dance of the future should convey with its slightest gestures some significance of the universe. The ineffable world of emotions and the glorious visions of the cosmos will be revealed through the medium of this language of divine beauty.

As we rise higher in the understanding of ourselves, the national and racial dissonances will be forgotten in the universal rhythm of truth and love. We shall sense our unity with all peoples who are moving to that exalted rhythm. Toward this joyous epoch the Divine Dance will add its own deep integrative force. Not by political or material changes, but by the unifying power of harmony will the world of humanity and nature be at One. The divine rhythm of creative love will flow in effortless ecstasy and beauty, encircling the world and embracing all humanity in one harmonious pattern of divine awareness and transcendent joy.

O dancers and lovers of beauty everywhere, I see a place of magical beauty, a world created of familiar things but arranged in new harmony and order!

I see children growing straight and proportioned, swift and sure of movement, having dignity and grace and wearing their bodies lightly and with power.

I see youth dancing in its exultant strength, triumphant in its dominion over the instrument of its body.

I see men and women moving rhythmically and with joy upon open hilltops bathed in the saffron rays of the setting sun.

I see them moving slowly with flowing serene gestures in the glow of the risen moon.

I see them giving praise—praise for the earth and sky, the sea, the hills, and praise for the omnipresent and eternal light.

Wisdom comes dancing…

Photographs

The photographs in this section and in the section
following Talks and Lectures are from the archives of
UCLA and the New York Public Library at Lincoln
Center.

Miss Ruth was the most photographed woman of
her time, and therefore the selection is huge. I tried
to pick some that showed her in a wide variety of
ages and poses. The first section shows her in her
early years. The second section shows her aging in a
beautiful and graceful way. If the names of the
dances are known they are given in italics.

Although photographs were not necessary to
illustrate the writing, I hope they give the reader a
feeling for this extraordinary woman. The credits for
the photographs are found on the copyright page at
the beginning of the book.

—KAM

Early Ishtar Pose

Ballet of the Zodiac

Wisdom comes dancing...

A Tagore Poem

Kwan Yin

Wisdom comes dancing...

A Movement Study at Jacob's Pillow

The Nature Sprite in Yosemite, California

Wisdom comes dancing…

With Pupils of the Denishawn School

An Impression of a Japanese Storyteller

Wisdom comes dancing…

The Yogi

The Yogi in later years

Wisdom comes dancing…

Section Two

Talks and Lectures

Most of the following talks on sacred dance were given by Miss Ruth at her Society for Spiritual Arts in New York City. Even though the first talk was the last chronologically, it is a succinct summary of her early inspirations on the subject. It was given at Jacob's Pillow in northeastern Massachusetts, a dance center founded by her former dance partner and husband, Ted Shawn.

—KAM

Jacob's Pillow - August 29, 1949

Rhythm and dance... visions of the immortal world... a solution to the "race" problem... spiritual dance... what is religion... spiritual autobiography... Church of the Divine Dance... Society of Spiritual Arts.

In its deepest sense, all movement in rhythm is religious, revealing in the body the cosmic eternal rhythms of the universe. The Hindus long ago set up the symbol of Shiva as the Lord of the cosmic dance because they knew that everything in the universe dances its way into manifestation. You and I are but specks of that rhythmic urge that is Brahma, which is Allah, that is God. But in reality we are accompanied by the whole dancing universe. We are fragments of the whole sport of Brahma. It is not a question of who dances, but of who or what does not dance.

In proportion to our realization of our own individual self as what the Hindus call Brahman, our senses will be enlarged and sensitized to a degree that we cannot yet imagine in our vision of the earth and stars. We will penetrate past the twilight images of our illusions. We will behold a fresh and light-filled earth and heavens—the same that Jacob came finally to behold.

These visions will not be intellectualized repetitions of our familiar earth and our familiar humanity, but will be the clear scene of a different kind of universe. It will be like when the mists clear in a valley and what appear to be unintelligible, unrelated objects become part of an intelligible whole. Right here where you and I stand, we shall behold a true and radiant world. In that world we shall dance only our joy and the releasing of our limitless Brahmanic selfhood.

There have been a number of painters who in their "second sight," of the world, as the Scots call it, have drawn for us inspiring, human, yet divine figures of pure dance, which are a stimulant to our minds and food for our souls. Blake, Doré and Fra Angelico are my favorites among the painters, with Flaxman's heavenly Greek studies, and Puvis de Chavannes of the French idealistic school, though there may be others you have found that I do not yet know.

These visionary painters have given us a line, a rhythm, an interrelationship to their human bodies that suggest the harmonious and immortal world. The world we all in our secret souls must believe exists somewhere, somehow, and to which we are all ascending the divine stairways. These painters stir our enfolded selves into a hope, a lift of the heart towards that ideal life of which all religions speak.

Ted Shawn and I were speaking lately about a certain meeting he attended that concerned what is called the "race question." The speaker before him was dwelling at ponderous length upon the various forms of government that were eventually going to bring, in his estimation, the much-talked-of harmony between the nations and the races. This was a long, involved process thought out by political minds. Then Ted arose and said, "But we at Jacob's Pillow have solved the race problem. We are not entangled in the frontiers and barriers of political schemes and ideologies. We meet in another dimension than that of slow-moving, combative forms. That dimension is beauty."

When I speak of the religious dance, I want so much that you will understand what I really mean. I mean a dimension of the free movement of our divine selfhood in any direction, in any posture, in any gesture or rhythm that releases our highest and most harmonious existence. Your rhythms and sacred cultural forms may be any spiritual tradition, symbolical or allegorical. You may individually find your own deepest spiritual strength and highest hope in the classical forms of the old, beautiful, Mother Church. This church has endured through the centuries, and its mass is one of the sacred and beautiful ballets in the world.

If you who have vague yet strong intuitive feelings that you would like to become a religious dancer, don't be delayed in your progress by feeling you must dance a Madonna or a Shiva or a Whirling Dervish or an old-fashioned Christian hymn just because someone else does. Not at all. Now I am going to put myself up as a fine target by attempting to define my concept of religion, though probably I'll be lucky if two of you understand and one of you agrees with me.

To me religion means the ceaseless search after perfection. It means my refusal to accept the limitations or evils of my life or the life of the world. It means to me the worship of beauty as the very face of God. It means that, as a very human being, I accept gratefully the wisdom, the discipline and the vision given to the world by the prophets of all ages and all races. It means that the scriptures of the world spoken or written by the people of life, versus the people of death, are my constant food, my daily refuge.

Religion means to me an abiding faith in God and humanity. It means a reverence for the Creator and the created, and a special dedication to holding high the dignity, beauty and immortality of humanity of which I hold the Dance as its greatest symbol.

Here is a brief personal spiritual history; all too much is already written about my factual history. I was born of a Methodist mother and an agnostic, Ingersoll-reading father, and what that makes me, I am still not too sure. [Robert Ingersoll (1833-1899), known as the "great agnostic," was a controversial orator who crusaded for a rational basis of human values.] When I was about twenty, I read *Science and Health* by Mary Baker Eddy (Christian Scientists please note that I am giving the author full credit) and with that book my whole outlook on life changed. Basically I have never left the principle of her Science from that day to this. I am like those little red dolls we used to see for sale on the sidewalks: no matter how many times you knocked them over they always righted themselves instantly. I am not what I term an ecclesiastical Bostonese Scientist, but no matter how many times I am knocked over, and they be not a few, I right myself by this revelation of principle given in this wonderful book. The core of it to me is that we actually, not factually, live and move and have our being now in a perfect spiritual universe.

More objectively speaking, all my life I read everything I could get my hands on of spiritual import. This makes me a grey sheep wherever I go. For I must now add that in 1936 (never question me closely about dates) in London I made my first contact with the Oxford Group. Through the personal greatness of Sam Schumaker of Calvary Church of New York City I became an Episcopalian, believe it or not.

Of course I am a grey-clad figure in his congregation too, because I still retain my metaphysical education. Probably Sam realized what I did need—that feeling of belonging—and in his rich, wide knowledge and love of humanity, he fed me the food I needed then.

Today I am the founder of my own small and growing church in California, The Church of the Divine Dance. This is an off-shoot, as it were, of my Society of Spiritual Arts, incorporated in New York City in 1934, and later in California. The bare facts of the activities of this tiny church are that we meet for meditation and prayer followed by our Rhythmic Choir practice on Wednesday evenings. Once a month we give a public rhythmic service. These services have been going on more or less continuously since the days of Denishawn House. How they began may interest you.

One night on tour in Beaumont, Texas, in 1927, Mr. Shawn had a birthday. We both felt at the time that we and our company had been too long away from our inspirational sources. Someone had just given Ted a copy of Ouspensky's *Tertium Organum*. We decided to gather for coffee and ice cream in Ted's hotel room. He would read us some pages from this highly exciting, if difficult, book. Picture Ted leaning against the foot of the bed, the rest of us spread around on the chairs and on the floor, feeling that something—we didn't know just what—had begun with his reading of this remarkable book.

We called it the Esoteric Society, and then as that seemed a bit precious, I later renamed it the Society of Spiritual Arts. Teddy became much occupied with other matters, including his mental blue-prints of Jacob's Pillow, and I went on with the Society by myself.

This brings me to the purposes of my Society and the Church. I have had a slogan for some years, which is: "We have the motivation of the church with the articulation of the stage."

Put as succinctly as I can, we want to mobilize the arts for religion. We consider our church a laboratory for the renaissance of all religious arts and new liturgical forms. Our plan definitely includes the expansion of equipment and a building, for the development and exhibition of the other arts, particularly the graphic. At present we exhibit drawings and paintings of a spiritual nature on our limited wall space. On our library tables, we have books of a religious and philosophic nature, dealing with the utilization of the arts as the instruments of humanity's highest realization. In our services, we use the poet, the dramatist, the actor, the philosopher, the musician and the dancer. In our organizational plans, we have definite national and international relationships established, so that in time we may become one vital agency for the moral and aesthetic education of world citizenship.

One of the specifics that we are interested in through research and daily practice is the *hasta mudras* of India as a new language for spiritual expression. I can remember the day when a hasta mudra had no meaning for practically the whole dance world. My own early career was not definitely concerned with this branch of Hindu dancing. There was no one in this country with whom I could study, and my dances were, as you now know, personal expressions of the Orient. With the coming of La Meri to New York City, I had my first real glimpse into the infinite possibilities of the mudra. When I was living at 66 Fifth Ave. in New York City, La Meri gave me my first glimpse of what can be done in the way of universal, silent language.

My goal in this regard is the translation into movement—using of course the total body, but with the accent on the hands—of the rich, poetic literature of spiritual realization.

Naturally a new terminology will evolve from this age-old and yet new relationship between the dance and religion. As some of you know I have dreams of a great temple, sometimes called a Cathedral of the Future, and sometimes called the Temple of Humanity. In this temple all the arts will be utilized to reveal the great spiritual laws of the universe and the beauty, inward and outward, of God's creation.

Lectures on the general theme: Dance as Worship

A series presented at the Society of Spiritual Arts in New York City

Wisdom comes dancing…

 *March 1, 1936*

Worship of the past vs. artistic creation... creation and passion... moral beauty and the body... the results of separating spirit from flesh... educating radiant bodies.

In looking constantly at the past for knowledge or inspiration, one is ever confronted with the effects and never the causes of those very examples which we so much admire. We see objects in pictures, statues and even the written word, of what the creating spirit of humanity has achieved in the past, but we do not contact the spirit. We see only its effects.

Worship of the past tends to develop the purely aesthetic qualities of the mind—appreciation, comparison, valuation—as opposed to the creative elements. Archaeologists, collectors, copyists or critical writers are rarely creative artists. Each phase of interest in past manifestations of beauty has its own value, but in this concept of the dance as worship it is its creative aspect that I wish to bring forth for special reasons.

In the physical world, the primary joy of the parent is in its own child, its own creation. Only secondarily is there joy in observing the children of others. In the world of artistic effort, however, the word *creation* has been too often loosely used. We may arrive at some measure of understanding by saying what creativity is not. It is not imitation, development, invention or rearrangement. It is not selection, adaptation or transmutation.

Creation springs from passion, the meeting place of the two creating elements of the Godhead, the positive and receptive, the male and the female. Creation on any plane and of any object springs from the same source, and if the dance is to be the vehicle and witness of humanity's spiritual development, it must cease saying "Lo, here and Lo, there," and must go upstream to its own dynamic sources of power and beauty.

The currents of traditionalism, whether in religion or art, always provide the safe and sane path for the masses to follow, to imitate or to adapt. The way of the pioneers, as of old, demands courage, devotion and a certain self-abandonment to where the spirit of inquiry or the spirit of creation takes them.

In this idea of the dance as worship, we lay the foundations for a new ecstasy and a deeper beauty in the dance for generations to come. We shall probably find ourselves in the dynamic disorders of all pioneering or creative efforts.

In all too many cases, the so-called healing (traditional or metaphysical) and moral regeneration of people of all kinds, ceases at the dissolving of some special sin or disease, while leaving the body as weak or ugly as it was before.

It does not seem to have occurred to many of the ministers of moral beauty or to the metaphysicians of mental enlightenment, that there still remains a whole range of healing to be accomplished before the individual bears and reflects in its entire body the fruits of its spiritual rebirth. It is here that the study and practice of the dance as a moral technique of life shall be part of the new age.

A woman's or man's body—its health, proportions and use—should, and as a matter of fact does, reveal plainly and often painfully the exact relationship that exists between the inward truth and the grace. Much of this lack of body beauty and body consciousness has grown from our theology and its insistence upon the separation of spirit from flesh. This false asceticism is also a dark strain running through even the more impersonal and metaphysical schools of thought. As long as any function or rhythm of the body is considered unclean, so long will we continue to regard the body with some measure of contempt and neglect. We then will suffer its disorders. It is not any part or function of our bodies that needs correcting, suppressing or ignoring but it is our concepts and attitudes of mind that need the deepest kind of moral cleansing.

We all need a new concept of our relationship to this instrument endowed upon us at birth. This holy, natural evidence of our spiritual poise and rhythm should be a part of our religious rather than our secular education, if we so divide them. Our clothes, climate, theology, social hypocrisy and evasions have all tended to beget in us a false and stupid attitude of mind towards the body.

All children should be encouraged to value the divine rhythms which pulsate through their radiant bodies. Every grown person should move with dignity and grace. I do not for one moment advocate swinging to the other extreme by making an idolatry and fetish of the body or of the dance. These are not things to worship in themselves or substitutes for the realization of ourselves as primarily spiritual beings. What I do advance is that we should bring our entire being—physical so-called as well as mental—in line with the divine will. Then the realization of life in its stupendous vibrations of power and beauty may find a pliable, exquisitely-tuned instrument through which to reveal itself instead of the dull, insensitive organism that we too often possess.

March 17, 1936

Dance as worship… body wisdom… body as instrument of worship… body of commerce and politics… sacrifice of the sacred self.

Perhaps it would be well to define to ourselves what we mean by worship. Fundamentally, is it an act of giving or receiving? Is it an act of acknowledgment or searching?

Perhaps in the course of a long and full life, one goes through all the stages of humanity itself in its so-called search for God. That is, one begins with fear and ends with love.

No matter how large and complex our religious institutions grow both in their organizational minutiae and in their beauty, there must be, as it were, a single cell from which the organism grows. That cell in its simplicity is covered, roughly, by the name worship.

My concept of the dance as worship must stem from that simple instinct, rather than from any of the advanced stages of humanity's expression in its later various developments.

It is my feeling that we should seek to recapture the actualities of rhythm as part of our future worship. Perhaps my most fundamental feeling is that, in using our entire body with all its capacity for expression, we at once cut to the root of our inveterate dualism.

As long as we are conscious of two entities, we shall continue to produce the kind of religion and the kind of ritual that we have today. I never fail to enter into one of our impressive and beautiful cathedrals without feeling sharply the substitution of human work for God's work as objects of our reverence and admiration.

We are invariably asked to admire architecture, painting, sculpture, music, oratory and costumes as evidences of our piety, but never the complete living body of humanity as the final expression of our realization.

The growing conviction of modern thinkers is that in all phases of this highly specialized civilization which we have evolved along lines of scientific discovery, religious organization and personal expressions of art, what we have left out as an object of our labor is the totality of humanity, our health and our happiness.

For over twenty-five years I have been saying and writing that I consider it a brand of insanity to send youth to college and to have them emerge at the end knowing about everything but themselves.

In the human body we already have the most marvelously complex, interesting, beautiful instrument and machine in the world. It is directly under our control, but as yet we know little about how to control it.

The ballet dancer, the acrobat and the body builder give us marvelous exhibitions of the control that will power can have over human muscles, but all of these forms of exercise are highly specialized and as a rule tend to be artificial. It is amazing what the human body can be forced to do. It is equally amazing how little idealization we have in regard to the totality of humanity and the body in particular.

Obviously, the Greeks had a higher ideal of the body and its possible development and perfections. They worked more intelligently towards the end of producing beautiful people than any nation I can think of. Hindu sculpture of ancient times also gives evidence of an admiration for the naked human figure, ornamented but not covered, as symbols of their highest states of realization.

As long as our passions for combativeness, competition and commercialism rule our ideas relative to all bodily forms of expression, we shall neither value nor evolve a perfect mind in a perfect body.

It is only by the restoration of our bodies as instruments of reverence, moral discipline and spiritual realization that we will set to work to evolve a finer life. On the one hand, we have the politicians and the representatives of the divine with corpulent or underfed bodies covered with the respectable black garments of their several offices, and on the other a well proportioned, beautiful athlete whose only concern is the body. We have women in all professions continuing to progress in heart and brain, but ignoring their bodies, while the ballet dancer's entire concern is with her arabesques and entrechats.

It is not that we should specialize less, but that we should humanize more. Our disintegrations show in our bodies as well as in our minds. What single act can polarize and focus the forces of life—physical, emotional and spiritual—like the dance?

Essential to the elements of worship has always been the sense of sacrifice or offering to God, apparently in exchange for benefits that God has or will bestow upon us. It seems that we are willing to sacrifice at the altar all things save ourselves. We give the first of the flocks, or the tithes of our income, but we do not consider the cultivation of ourselves in order to produce the perfect human.

I dream of a School of Wisdom where from childhood will be taught the sacredness of the human as well as of God. I see a ritual in the temple of the future which will present, for the joy of God and humanity, perfect examples of humanity's triune being—physical, emotional and spiritual.

Needless to say, when I use the word *dance,* I mean all postures, rhythms and gestures of beauty that can evolve as a language to reveal and manifest the soul's ascending states.

 # March 21, 1936

Dance as sacred ritual... spiritual and physical ideals... intellectual development vs. human self-knowledge... reassessing culture in light of body wisdom... "salvation" and dualism.

The conception and practice of the dance as sacred ritual should perfect the instrument of the body, as well as enlarge its range of experiences, and its entire need for expression. Therefore part of sacred ritual should be the demonstration of life—harmonious, beautiful, dynamic—as an ideal and as a witness of self-realization.

I foresee the possibilities of the dance being raised in its motivations to a higher level of consciousness, because greater beauty should evolve from it. This beauty should be an ideal for all to follow.

In the saints of all religions and sects we have had ideals of personal character, moral excellence and spiritual depth to emulate. From the great prophets and their disciples we have continually kept before our souls the spiritual person as an ideal of discipline and inspiration. When it comes to physical and artistic ideals of humanity, however, we have relegated their images to the art gallery, the stage and the boxing ring.

The church as such has had little or nothing to say about the physical body of humanity—its perfection or deformity, its usefulness as instrument of expression or its beauty as a delight to the heart and mind.

According to Ouspensky, it is impossible for us to grasp the totality of things with our mind. When we try to take in too many things we become bewildered and confused. If then we wisely retreat from trying to find eternity through the intellect, we will come, as it were, back into ourselves and there—by the simplest movement of breath in the body—we will at once fuse our inner and outer selves in a manner that no thinking can bring about.

The use of the dance with its infinite capacities for form, rhythm and beauty would be a test of a new viewpoint of civilization because it would withdraw the mind and energies to a considerable degree from the creation of a mechanical, artificial world. This artificial world now acts as substitute for the development and realization of our powers, as the automobile has deprived us of the joys of walking.

In his splendid book, *Man, the Unknown,* Dr. Alex Carrel points out that we have evolved through our intellects and inventive faculties an intense specialization, a world which is antagonistic to the entire well-being of humanity. He says, for instance, "In learning the secret of the constitution and of the properties of matter, we have gained the mastery of almost everything which exists on the surface of the earth, excepting ourselves" (p. 2).

Wisdom comes dancing...

It has always seemed to me a special form of mortal madness that we should expend the unbelievable amount of time that we do on every subject in the world except ourselves. We have bowed down to science as to a god, and being only half the truth, it has therefore proved not a god, but a devil.

Dr. Carrel further says, "Man [sic] should be the measure of all. On the contrary, he is a stranger in the world that he has created. He has been incapable of organizing this world for himself, because he did not possess a practical knowledge of his own nature. Thus, the enormous advance gained by the sciences of inanimate matter over those of living things is one of the greatest catastrophes ever suffered by humanity" (p. 27).

It is not that the specialized study of the human body and the dance, both in its present and as yet unexpressed possibilities, could give us the perfect realization of either our inner or outer life. The goal of perfecting the human body both as a manifestation and a symbol however would reorient practically the whole of human knowledge toward new patterns. The ideal of the perfected human would become the center or pivotal point around which inventions, arts, business and the whole minutiae of our objective life would function.

Thus the Divine Dance would cause us to reevaluate, from childhood to old age, past traditions and future inventions in the light of the full realization of ourselves. We have expended an immense amount of admiration and idolization upon our external existence in its manifold forms, but have conspicuously neglected the integration of the Self.

If we are to become artists in life, we must obviously have an ideal of perfection to work towards. Our religion in the West has held the word *salvation* as a goal towards which the entire instrumentation of the church is utilized. While our conception of salvation has, to some extent, drawn itself backwards from a future state to our present life, we have not yet divorced ourselves from the pernicious dualism which worships only the soul and leaves the body to companion with the world and the devil.

The dance is at once a creator and a destroyer of time. As Keyserling says in *The Travel Diary of a Philosopher,* the West is concerned with theological discussions and the East practices yoga.

 # March 26, 1936

Spiritual law and the body... an interpretive life... saving souls?... saving the body?... ministry to the lover and artist... naked body and religion... rhythms of time and eternity.

At present our understanding of spiritual laws is feeble, inexact and uncertain. Theologically speaking, our understanding has concerned itself largely with objectivity, with commandments relating to persons and things, but little with actual operation of spiritual law in relation to the body.

To have control over the elements of our lives, to control light in the midst of darkness, to bring beauty for ashes and order for discord, this is our need. I offer one answer to this need. Mine is essentially an interpretative life. I bid you come with me and sit at the feet of wisdom, the wisdom that has poured forth from the souls of the prophets of all times and races. Drink of this divine nectar, eat of this bread of true substance and be strengthened into power, into beauty, into love.

Wisdom comes dancing...

What we are in the temple is no different from what we are in the home and in the marketplace. We are truth and love in reality everywhere and at all times, but in the temple we focus our truth and love into terms of beauty.

As I think of the word *salvation,* a thousand challenging questions rise up in my mind. How can one save souls? Do souls need to be saved? Does one have to be sure that one's own soul is saved before one can presume to save others? What about the body, does that need saving, too? Are bodies and souls two separate entities, one to be saved and the other to be destroyed? Is there only one way of saving souls? The fundamentalists of each religion in the world firmly believe that there is only one way—their way. If the soul is saved once, must it be saved again?

Obviously, I can answer only a fraction of these questions to your or my satisfaction, for these are grave questions. Before I go on to attempt any answers, I should like to ask still others. Does not moral and spiritual healing, as we commonly understand it, also affect every atom of our bodies? Is it possible for us to be spiritually changed without being physically changed? In a word, we are a unity of being, and the changed states of our souls must affect instantaneously every vibration of our bodies. There is no such thing, therefore, as merely saving our souls.

My next question is, what part has beauty in the remaking of ourselves from discordant, unhappy persons into harmonious beings?

What prophet in these latter days has ministered directly to the lover and the artist, to those who create and who suffer in the regions of the heart, where in their emotional life the dreams of beauty and the longings of love are the scourge and the despair of their sensitive souls? Being a woman, I am concerned with these things. I feel that since they are the very stuff and form of life itself, our labor should go toward the understanding of the human soul and its illumination in perfect love and beauty.

I see the dance as instrument of worship in its two-fold meaning —first as manifestation and flower of the whole physical organism carried to heights of perfect coordination to which we have not yet attained, and second as a symbol, as Havelock Ellis says, "of being itself."

At present our use of the human body in all religious ritual and drama is fragmentary and incomplete, utilizing but a small measure of its full capacities for expression. In the first place, we are constantly substituting costuming for the body itself. Our climate, our customs and our clothing have all tended to make us afraid of the naked body in relation to religion. To be sure, we have sports where the body is revealed and used in healthful simplicity and grace, but we do not connect this realm of activity with our deeper states of spiritual realization. It is just at this point, even in the realm of the dance as it is popularly known, that we have what might be called "rhythms of time." What we need to find are the rhythms of eternity, the rhythms of Being itself.

In the body of a human, we see only the external form of the spiritual idea subject to limitation and distortion. In the symbolic sense, however, we may, by the right use of this body, convey some sense of its inner reality. This is the purpose and value of the Divine Dance, for not merely what you see and hear, but what you sense is the real meaning of the dance. It then becomes a communication of spirit to spirit by the medium of the body. Thought, emotion, realization, moods and emphasis, in their need to reveal or communicate, use the body as language; however, the body used as a life instrument, and the body used as an art instrument are two different matters.

We need purification of concept. All forms, elements, articulations and functions of the body must be regarded without coloring, that is without deification or degradation. As a life instrument, the body has the possibilities of a thousand delights that we are as yet ignorant of. As an art instrument, it has a thousand subtleties that we are as yet incapable of.

In that most exquisite of love songs, it says, "How fair and pleasant art thou, O Love, for delights." Thus speaks a friend of the Shulamite. "Who is she that looketh forth as the morning, fair as the moon, clear as the sun and terrible as an army with banners? How beautiful are thy feet with shoes, O prince's daughter. The joints of thy thighs are like jewels, the work of the hands of a cunning workman. Thy two breasts are like two young roes that are twins. Thine head upon thee is like Carmel, and the hair of thine head like purple. How fair and how pleasant art thou, O love, for delights" (Song of Solomon, 6-7).

 # March 27, 1936

Drama of awakening and the awakened... soul's conflict... solving problems with thought... revelation which restores and inspires... healing art and religion... ecstasy.

There will always be two phases to the Divine Dance or the dance as worship. The first is the drama of the awakening, and the second of the awakened. In the seemingly divided self, the battles between the real and the unreal will probably always be the most attractive for the common run of humanity. There is that in our constitution which demands combat. It all depends upon what we are combating, and "the warfare with oneself is grand."

Few saints are born and not made, or like poets, if they are so born, they spend long years in the mastery of their own gifts. Drama, which implies conflict and tension, has always held and will always hold the mesmerized attention of humanity. The interest and excitement of the soul's conflicts battling its own limitations should be a part of this worship through action. The second part—the awakening—infinitely more difficult—is also infinitely more valuable.

The dance of the awakening must evolve its own newness, rhythm and form. The old rhythms and the old forms will not avail. They were the language of the lesser self. In Fra Angelico's lovely *Dance of the Redeemed,* we find a great artist's conception of dancing in heaven. Here the freed souls and bodies move in the measures of eternity. They are moving and circling in another dimension, and joy radiates from their flying forms as they weave in the patterns of their Divine Dance.

The trend of our metaphysical age, in its religious aspects, creates a tendency to try to solve the problem of personality by thought. To be sure, a concept of truth, one's true being and one's relation to God must be held clearly and firmly in consciousness. To know truth's manifestation, however, to actually realize in flesh and blood the effects of this knowledge, we must learn to recognize the relationship between the soul and the body which so inextricably exists, and of which the breath is its symbol and sign.

In our universal view of truth, which is waiting to be discerned by humanity through the individual paths of salvation, there must also be a universal plane of manifestation, of health, strength and beauty. This concept of the religious use of the dance is an effort to turn our attention from the endless disputations and discussions of doctrine and theology to living, vibrant, imminent life, which is common to all.

Breath and food and movement is our common heritage. Our feet run on the earth, but our heads move in the air of heaven.

In these latter times what is called spiritual healing is being brought back into the universal consciousness. We are beginning to accept the idea that mind may control the body. We are beginning to study the technique of this vast subject and to realize that there are not two substances, mind and matter. But we are just beginning. We are groping towards uncertainty for we are dealing with the most illusive, uncontrollable element in the world, the human mind. At present we are intensely concerned with healing as the great center around which our mental activities revolve. This too often retards or limits our vision of a greater life.

It is this subtle limitation, this unconscious acceptance of life at a certain commonplace level, that causes quite instinctively the lover and the artist to mistrust what is generally called "healing." It is as if there were two phases to this revelation, that which restores and that which inspires. To the first belongs the destruction of fears; to the second, the revelation of beauty. Surely religion, from its complete and exhaustible nature should give both to its followers.

Healing as we generally conceive it is the restoration, the perfecting of the instruments of life, of body and mind, but it is not the playing upon the instrument. The person who makes violins and the people who play upon them represent two different stages of consciousness. Both are absolutely necessary for the expression of music. The realization of music itself is the basis or starting point for both the creation of an instrument and the technique of its playing. Music is a mystical, immaterial joy experienced by the human soul, but its manifestation must of necessity demand some form of instrument, some methods of playing. Both also demand certain grades of intelligence. So while we give all homage and credit to the maker of the violin, and to the teacher, yet our deepest joy and reverence goes to those composers and interpreters who have given us a sign and a foretaste of heaven's own language in the genius of their playing.

Now, this clumsy metaphor brings us at once to the profound and searching question: what is healing and what is the function of religion in the realm of art and inspiration? Are these separate or are they one? Is there healing and beauty? At once I can hear a thousand arguments of defense by patient and practitioner, that healing is a complete and radiant releasing of new vision and new life to those who are healed. Alas, too often, the healing proves to be but the mending of the broken instrument, a stringing of it up to pitch but no new song is played upon it.

Our human minds, once concerned with the dissolving of a specific error of mind or body, soon settle back into the routine of life as it has been lived before the extreme discomfort caused it to seek relief and control of its instrument once more. Being itself, however, has not learned to deepen its power of expression, to heighten its ecstasy of experience. This is what I feel should be the supreme function of the church. The church should be the stimulus and the technique of a greater life. There are new modes of life, new horizons of feeling that our mortal mind cannot picture. We think we know life because we know the small repeated rhythms of our common days, while all the while the very air is filled with heavenly music for our listening and a thousand new visions of life and love await our understanding and our courage.

In our efforts to do away with separateness, let us enlarge the borders of our world and allow healing to include the healing of dullness and stupidity, of narrow-mindedness and insensitivity, the healing of that deadness which is the negation of all higher beauty, the ignorance of all deeper bliss.

Wisdom comes dancing…

Photographs

Dignity in Aging

Gleaming Buddha

  Wisdom comes dancing...

Devotee in Prayer

White Jade—Dedicated to Samuel Lewis

Wisdom comes dancing…

Beggar for Beauty

Color Studies of the Madonna

Wisdom comes dancing...

Color Studies of the Madonna

He is Risen

Wisdom comes dancing…

With Company in *The Masque of Mary*
at Riverside Curch, New York

Dancer on the Mountain Top

Wisdom comes dancing…

Looking to the Future

The Prophetess

Wisdom comes dancing...

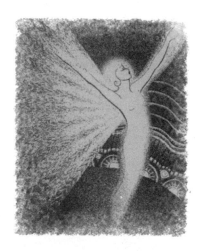

Section Three

Poetry

I. Embodied Woman as Divine

The Voice of Woman

I may be the Third—though indeed there may be others,

Deeper, greater, that are not yet known to the world.

I may be she who was to come

In this time.

It may be that, in my Mother's womb of love,

I was endowed in my hidden spirit

With powers and principles,

With qualities that I am only now becoming aware of.

There was a woman from Russia

Who had a vision and a purpose to reveal and revive

The ageless Wisdom—

Then there was a woman with the lamp,

From our Eastern states.

She wrote her Word and preached—

And begot a church which still grows and expands.

Then there is she who dances.

Behold indeed, "Wisdom comes dancing."

Have we not had enough of the minds of men?

The logical disputations and the sects arising from them?

Have we not had enough of the indifference

In the scriptures, to the life and need and wisdom of women?

They too were born and lived and inquired.

They too were found often in prayer and in the house of the Lord

Which they serve without reward of authority

Or a voice!

Too long has the Voice of Woman

Been silent.

Too long have the men alone sat upon the throne

Of the law—and spoken for all!

Now shall come—the Voice of Women—

And the child too shall speak

Wisdom comes dancing…

And then the artist shall sit in the chair of vision and creation.

And her voice shall be heard

Over the raucous voice of the demagogue.

Why always the Man Prophet?

Does not the woman, in the quiet hours of the night

Beside the bed of love and life,

Of pain and death—does she not often

Hear the still small voice of Wisdom, of Courage, of Joy?

In the midst of darkness—is this not also the word of

      Prophecy and praise?

These, the forerunners to the right ministry of beauty,

Have done and are doing their great task:

To leaven the seething of the world.

Verily, there is fighting in us also.

There is a planning and a vision and a fighting

For a just cause.

But with different ammunition and with different weapons

And a different battleground:

The battleground of the soul—where our own fears,

And the fears of our sisters over the earth, are vanquished

By the sword of the spirit wielded in prayer

Destroying our heart's enemies.

Truly we battle also—but in the soul—for victory

That our child may live, our husbands see clear again

And our own courage remain.

But these victories are not told

In great sonorous words.

They are not made into a great book.

Nor has her will been imposed upon the generations—

Rather she has been imposed upon.

Slowly she is rising to speak before the nations—

Before the parliaments—

Before the churches—

Before the world!

Wisdom comes dancing...

Her age is arriving—swiftly—powerfully!

The Age of Woman—Now—in the midst of the chaos

Of Godless worlds.

The Woman's Soul, breathing through the arts—

In the mercy tasks,

In the self-devotion—but not yet allowed

The Voice—the Plan—the Authority—before the world.

The New Scriptures,

The Women's Scriptures

Shall be written!

For the unborn—crying to them in the dark—

To awaken them from the dream of Man's will and ways and defeats!

December 28, 1946

My Mother Calls Me

My mother with brown skin and green hair.

My mother, warmed by the sun,

And illuminated by the moon.

I long to lie on her breast

And tangle my fingers in her hair, which is the grass.

I long to look up into the blue through the stiffened

      black branches of her trees in autumn.

And through the pale green tapestries of her springs.

My mother calls me and says, "Child, you have been

      too long in the cities, you have walked

      too long on the hard pavements, which are ever

      between your naked feet and my life-giving path.

Return to me and I will show you Heaven brooding over us

      in the fathomless blue.

I will heal you with my warm sense, and will rock you to

sleep with my tall pine trees murmuring their

twilight symphonies.

Come and live with the creatures whom I hold forever in

my eternal Heart—the birds and the little

wood animals and the friendly dogs.

They will not question you and the cat who royally

decorated your hours.

Yes, yes, you may return to the cities, you may get hard

work to do,

For the passionate ones who like yourself cannot rest.

Now come and live in me awhile and I will whisper to your

questioning heart of the deep peace of the limitless.

Rest, rest a while in my arms, my child."

December 21, 1947

White Jade

I am now on the Altar of Heaven at Peking.

Around me are the elements of nature, earth, fire, water, ether.

In me are the elements of Tao, the age-old "way to the eternal."

I gaze upon the outer world of mountains, seas and plains

      with understanding eyes.

I listen to the music of the stars, the low murmur of the waters,

      the soundless humming of the silent air.

My breath is the rhythmic evidence of unseen life!

I move to the rhythms of the drums of heaven.

My feet are weaving out the measures of eternity.

My own body is the living temple of all Gods.

The God of Truth is in my upright spine.

The God of Love is in the heart's rhythmic beating.

The God of Wisdom lives in my conceiving mind and

      in my constructing hands.

The God of Beauty is revealed in my harmonious body,

And the God of Joy flows forth in endless patterns of the Cosmic Dance.

I am Kwan Yin, the Merciful, the Compassionate.

All men and women, and children and all beasts, all creeping creatures and

      all flying things receive my Love,

For I am Kwan Yin, the Mother Merciful, who hears and answers prayers.

The Mother of the World

(She sits in a vast blue veil, holding the Babe of Light in her arms, as in the Nicholas Roerich painting.)

She loves!

The Divine Mother of the World,

Holding the Babe of Light in her arms.

She watches!

Mother of Creation,

She watches the glory of humanity

Unfolding its heart,

For these are her children.

She gives!

Mother of Life,

She gives her being,

Ceaselessly, eternally.

She sends forth!

She offers the Christ Child

To the world,

Endlessly blessing,

Healing and lighting all

Shadows in hearts.

Mother of the World

We salute thee,

We praise thee,

We love thee,

Mother of the Heart,

We adore thee,

We reverence thee,

We surrender our hearts.

Mother of the Body,

In rhythm and in praise,

We bring our lives to thy hands,

And our Divine Dance to thy feet.

Hathor

Hathor! Isis of the evening sky;

Goddess of the silver disk and outstretched wings,

Renew my soul—

Give me of thy magic life.

O sister of Osiris of the fields of peace,

Queen of Heaven, Beloved of the two lands

Give me of thy beauty

And thy love

Hathor! Hathor! Hathor!

Mystical

I am the woman soul

And I have come when you need me most.

I am the answer to your cry

And the deep need of your heart.

I come in the name of beauty

And in the purposes of love.

In one hand I carry the chalice of love

And in the other hand the sword of truth.

Sometimes I hold high the lamp of illumination

And sometimes I open the book of wisdom.

I am here appearing in answer to your

Utmost need.

Lift up your eyes and you shall see,

Listen with your ears and hear, understanding.

In some hours my voice is gentle with entreating love.

In other times it is terrible

With thunderings of healing truth.

Beloved children, are you ready,

Ready for the hour of rebirth?

Are you eager and willing to enter the Divine Life

From the death doors of mortal sinning?

Are you ready for the change,

The awful change from dying into living?

Do you believe in the eternal goodness

In the immortal light

In the rhythms of love?

Are you prepared to be burned and shriveled

And stripped and cleaned by the fire of Truth and Love

Made manifest?

Will you destroy without mercy

And pursue without pity

The wars and evasion in the dark domes of your ambitious minds?

I have overcome the ages and I have come to the

Threshold of your hearts.

I am creative love

Defying lust.

I am healing judgment,

Compassion and power.

I am an avenging fire and a renewing flame.

I am the woman soul

And I have come for your need

For your deepest need

Which is healing and light.

May 21, 1941

II. Dancing the Divine Dance

Temple Vision

Turning! Turning!

In the Divine Dance of ecstasy.

Our Arms are the thousand-petaled lotus of your perfect law

Unfolding, uncurling, weaving, waving

In the golden hours of nirvanic bliss.

Dancing, dancing in the ceaseless rhythm of the stars

Whirling in the azure spaces of the soul

Moving to the unheard voices of the suns.

Turning, turning,

Swinging, swinging,

Dancing, dancing,

Endlessly!

I see a Temple standing in the sun, white without and beautiful with

opalescent tints within. Alive, alight, aglow with the radiated rhythms of the

soul. Christ's heavenly kingdom is revealed and nirvana taught as end of long

obeisance and peace. Isaiah sees his visions come to pass and Mohammed

glories in his deep surrender to the One.

All Marys of the world await the Annunciation of the angel, bringing Bliss and the knowledge of their own creating being in the plan, as Parvati to Shiva long ago.

Here shall unfold the drama of the soul's need to know itself and God. First bewildered fears, lust and fighting and all the terror of the dream. Then surrender! The terrible triumphant dying of the lesser self, that it may shed its soiled, wrinkled skin and come forth whole!

Teachers of the Law, technicians for the manifested Way. Actors, singers, poets for the plays of the Way which have pain and wild dreams in their opening acts and peace and beauty for the epilogue.

The Divine Dance of Creation forever unfolding in the sacred bodies of Man and Woman! Patterns of Divine geometry drawn by living Dancers on the floors of the temple courts and made plain on the altar screens for all to see.

Our Eternal Parents

We are the inheritors

Of our Heavenly Father

And our Divine Mother.

Our emotions and our intelligence,

And our immortal souls

Are the raying forth in time and space

Of this divine inheritance.

We live under the eternal Law

Of our Heavenly Father,

The Law supreme which knows no deviation.

And we move under the protection

And love and beauty

Of our Universal Mother,

The fount of all compassion.

We are sustained by them.

We are guided and fulfilled by them.

We need not fear.

Our birthright is secure.

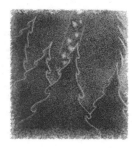

Prayer for Artists

O, Divine Father and Mother,

Makers of heaven and earth,

Supreme artists of creation,

I, thy humble instrument

Kneel here at Thy feet.

I listen for Thy inward word

And I wait to behold Thy inward vision.

Cleanse Thou me

From all sin and self-righteousness

From all illusions of prided vanity and fear.

Make me sensitive to Thy sounds,

To Thy vision, and to Thy rhythms.

Wisdom comes dancing…

Let me express beauty,

The wonders of Thy universe

And the immortal glories of my own soul

Which Thou hast given me.

Allow me to enter into that temple

Not made with hands

Wherein I may express the beauty of love

And the majesty of truth.

In humble and surrendered gratitude

For life, for love and for wisdom

I offer again and yet again

To Thee, my heart, my body and my mind.

November 1936

The Image Eternal

Oh, lovers of the dance,

And you who worship music,

And living forms of sculpture

Or the painter's skill in art,

Cease with me an instant

From your labors in the studio,

In theater or in concert hall,

And let us listen for an interval

To the Eternal Music,

And inwardly behold the Perfect Image.

And then let us begin to move

To the silent drum beats

Of the Perfect Dance.

The Kingdom Within

This is my message, the message of a dancer:

May you cease from creating a world of lifeless machinery,

And learn to use your own living instrument of beauty.

Cease from your pride of material conquest and accept

      your own inheritance of wealth.

Within your being, within your heart and mind and living body

There lies a kingdom that you little know of,

A world of fearless living, of power and of peace and joy.

A kingdom rich with love's glad sharing,

The unfolding glory of your Infinite Being!

How Beautiful the Mountains

You who worship music, or the painter's art, cease with me an instant from your labors in studio and theater, workshop and concert hall. Let us listen to the Eternal Music and inwardly behold the Perfect Image. Let us move to the silent beats of the Perfect Soul Dance.

For this is my message, the message of a dancer.

Within your being, within your mind and your living body,

      lies a world of joy and power.

Within you lies a kingdom that you know little of.

The kingdom of fearless living, of sharing love, and the unfolding glory

      of your infinite being.

All this and more is yours.

Cease from creating a world of lifeless machines and learn how

        to use your living ones.

Cease from your pride of conquest and learn to realize

        your inheritance of joy.

Dance in the morning — Dance in the night,

The dance of victory and joyous praise.

Let your children dance and your aged dance. Let all things move in the

        rhythm of Life. Let us dance alone and let us dance together!

Bending with the tides and swinging with the stars.

Beating with the heart drums and running with the winds.

For visions will come and powers will expand.

Love will renew itself and the mind grow clear.

O Dancers of earth in the East and the West, tell the spirit's meanings with courage and love. In the temple of old, they had a saying "They entered as humans and left as gods."

Our task is for beauty, for freedom and joy.

We begin in self-limiting, we end as light.

We begin in art worship, we end in God's prayers.

For our dancing feet bring peace and rhythms of another world. Our moving arms cast the sun rays in gestures, uplifted and wide. Our bodies move in rhythmic spirals, powerful and free. For we are the dancers upon the mountain.

Come and join us now, for we bring peace in beauty of the dance, Divine and Free.

This poem begins with page two and seems to be a combination of the previous two poems.—KAM

Wisdom comes dancing…

III. The Body as a Spiritual Messenger

Psalm of the Body

We praise the sun and the earth and the stars.

We see in them the works of the Almighty.

In the brightness of the glorious sun,

In the pale beauty of the moon,

In the deep azure of the sky,

And in the rhythms of the sea.

All these are worthy of our praise,

Should we not much more give praise for the marvels of our body?

The wonderfully wrought instrument of the soul?

Surely the perfect body is worthy of all honor:

Its efficiencies, its beauties—

Should not these be worshipped as well as all other parts

And wonders of the universe?

Behold the Head!

How wonderful it is, how it contains the five senses of our contact

       with the world—

The temple of the mind set on the column of the body—

What more worth to honor than the brows of wisdom?

The Arms and Hands,

How strong, how supple and delicate,

And manifold their uses.

The Torso!

How it contains the intricate organs of our breath

And the marvelous functioning of the heart,

Shall we not stand in admiration before the wonder of the spine,

That perfect tree?

And shall we not bow deeply before the breasts of sustenance?

And the Loins!

The instruments creating life, from the world invisible.

The Legs—

The firm supporters of all the Building.

And the dancing feet of joy

Are the pilgrims ever going to and fro.

All these are worthy of our praise,

This wonderfully wrought instrument of the soul.

March 13, 1936

I Preach to the Congregation of My Nerves

I preach to the congregation of my nerves,

To the lay brothers and sisters of my body.

I say to all the vast complicated citizenry of my torso,

"Thus shall you be moved and to this end."

I explain patiently to my muscles that of themselves

They cannot move, that all the useful and lovely creatures

Of my legs and arms are but clumsy reflections of my joy.

And to my head, the proud head, that is so certain of

"Its sovereign power to create," I speak sternly and say,

"Head, bend low in reverence, listen for the inner word

That is waiting to command you.

Look with wide surveying eyes

For the meaning of the turning earth,

That your multi-millioned atoms called brains,

And your ears, eyes and tongue

Are but the instruments for Mind to speak through."

I preach to my whole body

As to an unruly congregation,

Holding itself in groups and mobs, as not subject to the Law.

That self-delusioned ruler of this people of my blood,

The breath, I command in quiet, clear words of Light, that

It obey in silent, effortless rhythm,

The pure reflection of my harmonious will.

I say to my blood, "The circulating stars

Are not more certain of their way

Than your ceaseless moving universe

In the tracks and orbits of your world."

To the total members of this body,

Waiting like obedient slaves to do their

Master's will,

I illumine their weight and thickness

Of earthly concepts

By the knowledge that their entire form and outline

Is but the useful idea and substance

Of One governing Mind.

The Gates of Death

Through the insubstantial pillars of the gates of death

I shall dance my way to heaven

And the Elysian fields of the soul's free state.

For the dark portals of negations

Are but the shadows of my fears,

While the radiant rhythms of my Dance Divine

Shall dissolve and scatter these

As I enter the Perfect Day

Treading the measures of the stars.

IV. Poems That Inspired Dances

The Ballet of the Beloved

This is the Ballet Dance

Of the Beloved,

The singing of his light,

The loving of his love.

These are the words of his wisdom

And the rhythms of his life.

This Ballet is the going forth by day

And the returning home by night.

These are the gifts of his giving

And the pouring of his wine.

By these are we scourged

And chastened for his sight,

From his right hand they emerge

And to his left hand they return.

They move in his measures

Yet visible to the world.

They are the thought forms of his pleasure

And the arrows of his will.

December 26, 1934

Wisdom comes dancing...

Siddhas of the Upper Air

In the blue spaces between the stars

The Siddhas stand together.

Blown by the lifting winds of the whirling worlds

They move side by side with the effortless motion of the

Divine Dance.

Gazing ahead their hearts beat to the

Unearthly rhythm of perfected love.

They are moving towards the light of the unimaginable sun.

And their garments are blown behind them

Like a comet's saffron tail.

October 7, 1930

The Prophetess

(A feeling of the old prophetess somewhere in it—a prophetess of Beauty.)

I was born to know Beauty—

The love beauty...The nature beauty...The body beauty

The god beauty...The art beauty...The machine beauty

The love beauty is always the same and yet not the same.

It is the beauty of the whole earth reflected in your eyes.

Through the translucent touch of your tender hands

I feel the whole delicate splendor of the sun.

Through the long, searching gaze of your eyes

I feel the infinite love knowing of the world

of endless centuries, both ways of time.

In the love singing tone of your voice

I hear the cosmic love music between the stars.

I prophesy of beauty beyond the world's twilight singing.

I prophesy of splendor beyond the centuries to give.

I prophesy of love filling the world with bliss.

I prophesy of knowledge of inner dreams.

I prophesy of life infinitely lived.

I prophesy of God in whom I am reborn.

I sit here amidst the cross-ways of the world listening for the Word.

I am the daughter of the generations past

And child of unknown time—Egypt and the Pyramids.

I am the fulfilling of the dreaming dancers of the temples of the sun.

I am the dream of nations that are waiting for release.

I am the messenger of heaven sent to dance "The Dance!"

My soul is an Aeolian harp, swept by the winds of heaven.

I am singing songs of silence that are beautiful beyond understanding.

The prophetess sees a vision of body alone or in illumination.

She sees how the soul is purified, how the Self

Of humanity must be tried

And tested, tempted and released.

She sees that on the mountain top of spiritual ecstasy.

She is caught up in the spirit.

When you approach nearest the Divine principle

do not be surprised that you must share the hemlock cup!

This is my sermon.

I am one who cannot by her very destiny give forth day by day, but must posit her realization ahead of her in time and then when the hour shall come this soul shall breathe forth its ecstasy.

October 28, 1930

Wisdom comes dancing...

I

Am

Brahman

Turn away, turn away

From the sights of evil thoughts made manifest;

Turn away from the vile curiosities of vile deeds.

To turn the gaze from the objective, illusory universe inward upon the self is

made possible by the Hindu wisdom and symbology.

I Am Brahman

This becomes at once the focus, symbol and manifestation of the self.

I Am Brahman

This is to become conscious of one's entire organism, so-called physical, emotional and mental manifestations, in perfect alignment, and perfect functioning posture. Thus one has the sensation of drawing upward from illimitable depths, and downward from unmeasurable heights, one's power. To all points of the compass, one becomes aware and awakened. At last the soul is freed.

At last the illusions of the misbegotten conceptions of the world are dissolved and utterly destroyed. One stands free and complete, ready to manifest rhythm in joy, and all things that have been latent in the soul since the beginning of the illusion of time are revealed.

I Am Brahman.

This contains all governments, all sciences, all arts. In this single self, without a second, complete in its balanced faculties and elements of the masculine and feminine selfhood, desiring nothing, and needing nothing this self is awake and aware of its own supreme intelligence, its own immortal, limitless being, forever unfolding in delight, all arts, all sciences, all government.

Wisdom comes dancing...

This is the supreme Divine Dance towards which all dance aspires.

I Am Brahman.

This is the end and the beginning of all paths of wisdom, all understanding of the gods and God.

This is the embodiment of the Law. The perfect, frictionless, harmonious, ever-present Law.

Thus we become the eternal lotus ceaselessly unfolding its leaves, ceaselessly producing its own seeds in the silent rhythm of the Law. The Self emerges slowly or swiftly, harmoniously or painfully, becoming only the witness to the shedding of its lesser selves, one by one.
The Self emerges swiftly and harmoniously from its binding sheets.

This Divine activity is to shine, to dance in silent bliss. To share, to give to all of life in the three worlds: past, present and to come.
To share with all areas, all levels of mineral, animal and human life, seen and unseen, the living and the dead.

I Am Brahman.

This Self therefore, is the knowledge of Brahman, the death and the resurrection, the lesson learned, and the lesson taught, the worship and the worshipped.

This is Brahman.

March 6, 1950

Wisdom comes dancing...

The Lamp

During the night of death the divine star of life appears, giving forth its rays

of illumination and release.

In our youth we see only the day star of the sun.

In the warmth and light of this invisible symbol

We rise upon our feet and live out our youthful days of divided life.

Long before the Son of Righteousness appears upon the horizon of the soul

We yearn for beauty, for love, for truth,

We search here and there upon the earth,

We question ourselves,

We lift imploring hands to the unresponding sky,

We are lost in the mazes of life.

There comes upon us, in season and out of season,

The veiled light of the soul.

But we are not yet awake—and cannot see.

Later the first breath of the approach of death brings a chill to our hearts.

We protest our willingness to die, we refuse our consent

To this great and terrible image of darkness and despair.

We are overwhelmed and yet we still believe,

We are dying and yet we still live,

We run to and fro and bewail the hour of our birth,

Since it has led us to this wall!

We are frozen into a dreadful plastique of horror and despair.

Death has arrived.

But behold!

The hope and faith of all the ages has not failed.

For there upon the high horizon of the soul

Appears the night lamp of eternity.

The dreadful darkness is illumined—

The strange and terrible shapes of our own imaginings are slowly changed.

The light has come.

She who brings the lamp of perfect life

Gives of her light to those who desire it with passion and with tears.

Those who struggle to attain are given the power of the lamp

To heal, to liberate, to love.

The veil of death is lifted part by part until its last full

Weight of earth is carried into the regions of the light

And there destroyed.

Love and beauty are resurrected from the burial of time and space.

The ascent of the soul goes on.

New heavens are revealed.

The dance of those who are free is like

The feet of those upon the mountains who

Bring tidings of peace and great joy.

February 12, 1942

Expanded version. A brief version, starting with "She who brings the lamp," appeared in *Lotus Light*, page 75. —KAM

Wisdom comes dancing...

*A Series
of Drawings
by Ruth Harwood*

Ruth Harwood, an artist and
dear friend of Miss Ruth's,
illustrated Miss Ruth's book of
poems, *Lotus Light*. These
drawings are a selection from
that book. Since we could not
locate more drawings and it
was Miss Ruth's wish to
illustrate her book of dance
with Ruth Harwood's drawings,
I decided to use these as a
fitting tribute to a remarkable
artist.

—KAM

Mountain Of Vision

A Series of Drawings by Ruth Harwood 165

The Soul

  Wisdom comes dancing…

Crusader

A Series of Drawings by Ruth Harwood 167

Lotus Light

  Wisdom comes dancing…

Forest Mood

A Series of Drawings by Ruth Harwood   169

Ascendancy

Wisdom comes dancing…

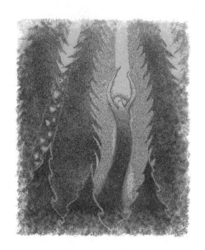

Section Four

Other

Writings

Some of the following writings
on various topics are not fully
developed, but they show the
variety of Miss Ruth's interests.
The first essay was a proposal
for a temple of arts at the 1939
World's Fair, where dance could
be seen as a divine pursuit.
Although the building was not
built, Miss Ruth and her
Rhythmic Choir did perform at
the World's Fair.

—KAM

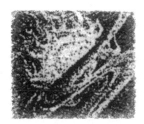

I Would Build A Temple of the Dance

I would build a Temple of the Dance...

Where all manifestations of human rhythm may find adequate expression...a Temple dedicated to this age-old art, which is now having its renaissance in America...a Temple that America can be proud of—beautiful, dynamic, progressive and educational. The only theater in the world where the spiritual vision of life will have expression in terms of pure beauty. A Temple which is the meeting place of church and stage, of life and art. Where newer and keener appreciation of the dance not only as one of the great arts, but as one of the natural expressions of human life will take place, because lectures and other mediums of interesting education will enlighten people as to what the dance really is.

The century of progress in America includes the phenomenal rise of the Dance as one of its cultural and educational phases.

Why is America dancing and inviting the world to dance with her? Because at this time in the history of America, she desperately needs the power of spiritual realization and expression to oppose the expanding forces of materialistic tendencies, expressed in business without love, war without mercy, and machinery without morality.

All spiritual channels of expression need to awaken to the responsibility that is theirs, to offset the speed and suicidal concepts of material existence. This theater of the dance, this theater of the divinity of rhythm, will provide one vitally interesting place in the World's Fair, where the thousands may feel their senses and their souls refreshed and revitalized by the power of spiritual realization in action.

April 9, 1932

Wisdom comes dancing...

I Demand of the Dance

I demand of the Dance—more than any of the other arts—that it reveal the God in humanity—not merely the scientific and beautiful forms that the body can be made to assume, but the very divine self.

I demand of the Dance—as it sweeps through the centuries—that it leave a noble influence in the race that evolves it, and not only the clever and brilliant record of its human actors.

I demand of the Dance that through it the visions and ideals of humanity find expression and not merely its ephemeral and distorted concepts.

The Dance should be the first and most inspiring of the human arts. It should be held responsible for the health, beauty and moral balance of the race, for it is the business of the Dance to lead and not to follow.

The Dance should not be content to merely reiterate the errors, evils and grotesque obscenities of its contemporary life. To be sure these matters now occupy the thoughts of the amusement world. They will continue to occupy the thoughts of part of the world always. But if the Dance is to sweep down the years, leaving a lasting beauty and brightness in its path; if it is to have its part in pressing back the animality and confusion of the world, its leaders will have to have a greater torch than can possibly be lighted from a concept of mere mechanical proficiency.

For when the Dance has merely reflected the superficial life and customs of any given generation, expressed in its passing fashions and limited, ugly movements, it has followed its generation, not led it.

What the body of a human can do in its trained and athletic sense—jump, run, leap, turn, spring—these are all interesting and beautiful exhibitions of the body as a physical instrument. To call these and all other evidences of mere physical prowess "the Dance," however, is to at once belittle and circumscribe the true meaning of the word to the mental limitation of a particular school.

All gestures, all technique, all inventions, all varieties of motion that we now know—and those yet to be unfolded—are the bodily words needed to tell the story of the human's active and inquiring mind

April 1925, New York

The manuscript ends here with a cliffhanger note: "Find Missing Page."
—KAM

Dance the Divine Dance: An Esoteric Credo

There is no place for error of any kind in my affairs: in my heart, its motives, in my mind, its devisings or in my environment.

I am the instrument and the embodiment of good. I am complete and harmonious in my operations. There is no personal I, there is only the reflection of invisible, indivisible Intelligence.

I am being used in the great pattern of the divine will: to radiate life, strength, grace, beauty and form. My work is established: it is posited on the Eternal and cannot be moved or destroyed.

I am in my rightful environment now—the environment of affirmation, receptivity and cooperation. Every instant I am aware of my indestructible relationship to Mind and its reflection. I live, dance and have my being in the Realization of my immunity from all entangling limitations and distorting influences. My work is to reflect intelligence, life and beauty. My relationships are maintained by love and not by fear.

I am ready at any moment to learn, to practice, and to express. I am necessary to the complete expression of the One governing Mind. In proportion as I maintain my own true individuality, I add to the variety and beauty of the world's manifestation of Life.

I Dance the Divine Dance

I begin my Divine Dance by clearing all mental limitations, unnecessary objects, all confusions and myself.

I move in space and I move in light.

I move in rhythm, in form, and in color.

I bring the instrument of my body to its rightful environment, where I listen for the inward music.

I wait for the urge of spiritual joy, happiness and beauty to move me.

I am conscious of myself as reflecting in posture, movement and design the one creative mind.

I am not a creator—I am a reflector.

I am not an originator—I am an interpreter.

I am not a material body—I am a spiritual consciousness.

Society of Spiritual Arts

In response to the idea of using dance in traditional worship, there came to
our services at the Temple Studio many persons of various ages, well-trained
and those who had never done any classic dancing before. After a few weeks
of practice in the simpler forms of movement, it became necessary to divide
the group before attempting the more complicated rituals.

We divided them into three divisions: The Altar Choir, The Rhythmic Choir
and the Dancing Choir.

The Altar Choir consists of those who have never danced in our meaning of
the term, and the more mature persons. Their duties are to arrange the altar
properties and to take part in certain simple rhythmic movements connected
with the ritual.

The second group, the Rhythmic Choir, has as its members those who have
had some dance training and whose physical suitability warrants their use in
the dancing of hymns and other phases of the service.

The third group, or Dancing Choir, is composed of well-trained dancers who
are capable of the more technical expression of the service.

Credo for the Rhythmic Choir

As priests of this Temple we hold ourselves in readiness to translate and interpret in terms of rhythm, tone, color and form, that body of truth that is understood by us and capable of being given in terms of art.

1. We observe that life is a great moving ritual from birth to death.

2. We understand that humans are the universe in microcosm.

3. We accept the spiritual viewpoint of life as opposed to the atomic or materialistic.

4. We know that we are surrounded, supported and governed by Infinite Life.

5. We endure the burden of renunciation, purification and labor that the flame of beauty may be kept perpetually burning upon the altars of the world.

6. We feel that we emerge into light through wisdom, through love and through suffering.

7. We seek to understand the stages or states by which the soul of individuality is purified and exalted.

8. We are dedicated to the realization and interpretation of life as spiritual, harmonious and eternal.

9. We agree as a working principle of art, that no manner of expression, no technique in itself, is of value in this Temple, but all technique is of value, in so far as it surrenders itself to the meanings of life.

10. Our language is the language of art in its totality, our bodies being the beginning and final instrument of expression.

11. Our spiritual and artistic ideal is the Divine Dance in which all action and elements of our being are caught up into a unity of beauty.

Fixed and Standard Principles for Religious Dance

There is a great distinction to be made regarding all religious dancing on the following matter:

God gave humans the ability to sing. They sang in their own personal, outpouring manner—individuals alone—long before we had the science and art of singing. Nevertheless, partly for preservation, partly to set up a standard for all students of music to follow, we now have text books on the teaching of basic principles. We also have the written compositions of the masters. These two seemly antagonistic elements can be found in the dance, as well as in music. When they are studied certain conclusions follow.

I am persuaded that the natural rhythmic movements of childhood are implanted by God in every child along with their very breathing. These impulses to dance are indeed individual in each child and should be respected as such in the teaching of children. At the same time we come at once to the fact that there are instinctively basic principles of balance, sequence, repetition and imitation of the natural world that are found in each child's dancing. This being so, in our more adult development of this art, we must take elemental spiritual facts and impulses for our consideration and not only our natural desire to move in rhythm.

I have heard the most glorious improvisations by very sound and cultured musicians. Their mood of a great sense of freedom in giving forth music, what the Greeks called their *daemon*, seizes them. I am sure that they let through some of the finest music that they ever produced. Let us remember that inspiration comes through the human mind in two definite ways: one by unprepared exultation, which possibly may never be put down on paper. In another method or manner musicians hold themselves over a long period at the command of the spirit of music, by which they finally give outer form to their great symphonies.

As the percentage of deeply creative people whose work is known to the world is small and the multitude depend for their moments of great joy upon these few, there has to be a medium of expression which remains more or less fixed and standardized, for the many to learn from and be guided by. This will definitely apply to the religious dance and all its forms.

We shall range from simple fixed standards of movement on up to greatly personalized ecstatic movements of praise or exultation by the dancer who has consciously or unconsciously obeyed the laws of dance as the improvising musician obeys the laws of music.

Stabilization of the Dance

Similar to parts of "The Divine Dance":
perhaps an early form of these ideas.
—KAM

The stabilization of the dance does not mean a fixed principle, a teaching that there is one way to dance, but rather the making of a roadway, wide and level, over which may flow various forms of healthful and beautiful art; those forms that are now known and those that will evolve in the future.

Stabilization, however, does mean the statement of and adherence to certain standards of activity: standards of subject matter and standards of technique. These ideals are arrived at by processes of inspiration, experience and tradition, as well as by a constant inflow and outflow and by eliminating what is less and perfecting what is better.

Our aim is to sacrifice and conform on those sides of life that, as creative artists, we can conform and sacrifice on, in order to release and preserve those elements of our creative ideas that are personal and unique. We agree most thoroughly to the justice of personal recognition, that no individual composer or interpreter shall be taken for granted and smothered in the general statement of a performance.

All training from whatever school or person shall be given credit and acknowledgment where such acknowledgment is desirable and practical. Until we can evolve a clearer and better method of doing so, we shall borrow from our friends, the musicians, their immemorial method of stating sources of every dance creation on every program and in all matters where practical in relation to performance.

The prostituting of our art life has given rise to many evils. Like the prostitution of love, it has produced a great sterility in those who practice it and a general lowering of respect and admiration for art itself.

The essential first element of art expression is freedom. Freedom of mind, freedom of body and freedom of materials—that, is money.

If it be true that the kingdom of God is within us, and if it be equally true that all powers of heaven and earth are to be subject to the will of God, then surely the changing of the outer world into images of the world within by means of rhythm, proportion, form and color is the work of true salvation. This is the high duty of our race, the race of dancers, those who know they are the temple and the instrument of the living spirit. Also the veil and the door, but the veil must be rent and the door opened. But the substance of our veil of flesh is no more solid than the thickness of our ignorance.

The limitations of our senses are the grey stones of our prison walls. There is one way to escape—one way to enter the open country of the kingdom and that is to fly—to fly over walls with wings of spirit and in the ecstasy of what we see dance and sing our visions of the soul.

The dance is at once very old and very new—it is old in its past forms; it has always been used by the ancient race; its expression through rhythm is the cornerstone of all great arts that the body expresses. Today we are at the beginning of a great renaissance of the dance.

The dance is immortal—it can speak the message of spiritual power and beauty in terms of rhythm, tone and color better than any other means, for as Havelock Ellis says, "It is not only the supreme manifestations of physical life, but the supreme symbol of spiritual life."

The passing errors and vulgarities of humanity will be always with us. The children of this world will ever amuse themselves in their own way. But every hour souls, who have a natural nostalgia for the unearthly beauty of the Immortal Being, are born into the world. It is by these and to these that this ideal, these revelations of the spiritual consciousness, set forth in understandable terms of a three dimensional world, will be at once food and shelter to their spirit.

Wisdom comes dancing...

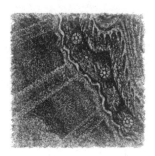

The Symbolism of Colors

Although, as Miss Ruth says, this piece is incomplete, I include it because it gives an insight into some of her thinking on color in costuming. —KAM

Since I have no knowledge of color symbols or psychology except my own instinctive feeling for them, I can only offer my own ideas on the subject. These ideas are based upon the effect that the three basic colors (red, blue and yellow) have upon me, and then considering the mixture of these colors in trying to decide the meaning of the other colors.

Red symbolizes the passion of the flesh.

Blue is the symbol of mentality or intellect.

Yellow is the symbol of pure spirit.

Since brown is attained by mixing all three of these basic colors, and matter is the result of the joining of carnal passions, mentality, and spirit, so brown is the symbol of matter.

Dark green is a symbol dominated by the intellect. It can be hopeful or degenerate, depending upon the intensity of the color. If the color is very dark, having more blue than yellow in it, it may symbolize the deep brooding types, possibly intellectual endeavor directed to unhealthy ends.

The lighter shades of green, having more yellow in them, symbolize lofty intellect reaching higher into the spiritual realms. Because green lacks red, the passion color, it is also a symbol of stagnancy in the deep greens and of calm in the light greens.

Orange (red and yellow) in its dark shades symbolizes the carnal passions in their most exalted state, when they are in complete harmony with the exaltation of the spirit. The paler oranges, being more dominated by the spirit, symbolize sublimation of the passions. Because of the lack of blue (the mental color) in orange, it is also a symbol of fanaticism.

White is the symbol of virginity. The white surface is ready to record any and all colors that contact it. It is not an entity, other than that of the most abject virginity, until it has been given character by the infiltration of other colors.

I realize that this is very incomplete and would like to go into the subject deeper as time goes by.

Radha: Delirium of the Senses

In order to protect her creative work, Miss Ruth wrote this synopsis of *Radha, Delirium of the Senses,* for copyright purposes. It was reproduced in Ted Shawn's book, *Ruth St. Denis: Prophet and Pioneer* (1920, pp. 30-31). —KAM

Scene: Interior of a Hindu temple

At the center back is a large niche and shrine in which is seated the image of Radha, cross-legged in the attitude of Buddha, before which incense is rising. At one side the temple caretaker kneels in prayer.

Curtain

Enter the first high priest at lower right entrance; he advances toward the idol carrying incense, which he renews before the shrine. He kneels in worship, then rising rings the bell at the side.

Enter the first temple servant, bearing a tray of garlands of flowers which the high priest takes and hangs around the neck of the idol, then he rises and strikes the gong suspended from an arch.

Enter the second temple servant, bearing loose flowers on a tray, which the high priest receives, scattering some over the idol, pouring the rest into a small dish at the foot of the shrine. He strikes the gong again.

Enter a pilgrim with an offering of coconuts, which the priest receives.

Then dipping his finger into the sacrificial paste, he marks the forehead of the worshippers with the sacred symbol. At this point all the bells and gongs loudly strike. All the servants, pilgrims and priests advance slowly upstage and kneel in front of the shrine, forming a semi-circle around the goddess.

After a short interval, Radha, partially hidden from view by the heavy clouds of rising incense, descends from her pedestal and, standing at the foot of it, gazes with benign countenance on the worshippers who draw back and prostrate themselves before her.

Radha then signifies that for a short time she has taken this form in order to give them a message. She bids them rise and receive this, which she then conveys through a mystic dance, the meaning of which is that they must not seek for permanent happiness in an impermanent world; that the quest for pleasure through the five senses always ends in unfulfillment; that peace is only to be found within.

The dance of the senses is comprised of three figures being performed in five circles one within the other, each circle representing one of the five senses. Each of the first four is symbolized by different objects: jewels for sight, bells for hearing, garlands for smell, a bowl of wine for taste, and for touch she kisses her own hands.

The second figure dances on a square representing, according to Buddhistic theology, the fourfold miseries of life, and is done with writhings and twistings of the body to portray the despair of unfulfillment. At the end of this figure Radha sinks to the ground in darkness.

After a short interval a faint light discloses her in an attitude of prayer and meditation. This light, coming from a hanging lamp of lotus design, is first concentrated on her figure, then diffused with increasing power over the entire stage. Radha now rises from a kneeling posture, her face illumined with the light of joy within, and, holding the lotus flower, begins the third figure of the dance, which follows lines of an open lotus flower, the steps leading from the center of the flower to the point of each petal. She dances on the balls of her feet, thus typifying the ecstasy and joy which follow the renunciation of the senses and freedom from illusion. At the close of this figure, which finishes the message, Radha, holding aloft the lotus flower, slowly dances backward to the shrine, followed by the priests, the curtain meanwhile gradually descending.

When the curtain rises, again, the image of Radha is seen seated once more in the shrine, her spirit having attained samadhi. The worship is over, the lights are out, the priests are gone, leaving the idol, alone once more, to the shadows and the silence of the temple.

Dancer at the Altar

A poetic dance description from
An Unfinished Life. —KAM

The Dancer comes to the Altar—The Dedication:

I, the Dancer,
Bring my Body
To the Feet of God.

The Dancer lies on the Altar—Surrender:

All rhythm, forms, and powers
Of my being
I lay on the Altar
Of the Cosmic Mind.

The Dancer kneels—Prayer:

O! Infinite Father-Mother

Of all living things,
Accept me as the Child
Of your Eternal Bliss.

  Wisdom comes dancing...

O! Infinite Creator
Of the turning worlds,
Use me in the Pattern
Of your Infinite Design.
Cause me to move
In the rhythms of Divine Creation.

The Dancer ascends the steps to the Symbol—Understanding:

In lines of Light
I behold the structure of all Designs.
In curves of color
I hear the sound
Of the Eternal Word.

The Dancer turns around from the Symbol—Realization:

I feel
Around me the spaces of Eternity.
I hear
The beat of the soundless Drum.
I stand
Bathed in the Light of distant Suns.
I turn
With the ageless rhythms of the Stars.
I touch
The etheric waves of Love.
I walk
In the measures of Eternity.

The Dancer steps down to the Dancing Space—Expression:

Look!

The World is filled with Light!

Listen! The Cosmic Drums are beating!

My Dance of Life begins!

The Dancer begins to move in the rhythms of the Divine Dance.

Alternate Preface for "The Divine Dance"

The following is from the manuscript of "The Divine Dance." It was written in 1960 and added to the original manuscript. We did not locate the drawings mentioned here. The drawings used throughout the book in piece form are presented whole in the Section preceding this Section. They are from *Lotus Light,* Miss Ruth's published book of poetry. —KAM

In presenting this book to all those interested in the subject of religious dancing, I can only say how very grateful I am to Adelphi College, where I am now artist-in-residence, for doing such a splendid job of mimeographing these pages.

This book was written at Denishawn House in about 1934 under the most valuable cooperation of the late Ruth Harwood, who not only typed these pages for me but intended to add to its ultimate publication some of her priceless drawings. Alas, this never happened. Ruth has left behind her many of her beautiful metaphysical drawings, with which I shall ultimately illustrate this book. I shall hope in the near future, to get a publisher to give this book its proper mounting. In the meanwhile, I shall hope that it will have some value to those students who are not only here at Adelphi College, but to other students in other colleges all over our country.

Last Chapter of "The Divine Dance"

Written at Adelphi College in 1960, this piece describes Miss Ruth's further projects at the time. —KAM

Today I feel that a great new experiment lies ahead of us which will be the silent language of the human body for translating thought and feeling into gesture and rhythm without sound.

To this end, all forms of meaningful gestures of the body would be called into play: the hasta mudras of India, probably the most complete hand-language in the world; all of the symbolic and expressive gestures of various races, and the new creative forms which inevitably arise from our own creative experiments.

Much excellent work is now being done in the field of new vocabularies of gestures; some with and some without inner content. Various schools are offering new methods of expression to children and youth to experiment with, both for performing and teaching. But I do not believe that very much has been accomplished by way of integrating the spiritual being of humanity with this new form of rhythmic expression.

My own studies until now have been concerned with traditional Western Christian art forms as guide and background to my Rhythmic Choir and seasonal pageants. But now, with the help of my young student, Barbara Andres, I am pushing into metaphysical dimensions of thought and action.

In this regard an occasion that made a profound impression on me was the appearance of a French dancer, unknown to me and the general public, who gave an extraordinary exhibition at the Metropolitan Opera House in New York City about thirty years ago. I think I got from her the word *metachory*. In any event, she used a large painted mandala for her backdrop. (A *mandala* is an Oriental symbolic design of spiritual meaning). On the floor, she danced on a replica of this design. The art of metachory is the rhythmic art of translating the abstract truth of being into the symbolic art forms of tone, color, rhythm and design.

In this manner, the dance becomes a language of silent speech, a translucence for wisdom to be intelligently communicated. Many years ago, I made some experiments with Doris Humphrey on what we called the "silent" dance, for I began to see that the rhythmic language of the body is not necessarily in need of sound.

Today, as "artist-in-residence" at Adelphi College, I not only have the opportunity to teach my classes the beginnings of their spiritually rhythmic education, but also continue to inquire and explore vast new areas of bodily expression of the divine self.

By way of a guide to profitable reading along these lines, I am preparing a useful supplement bibliography of books which have fed my own well-springs of thought and action. I can only hope these will feed and stimulate others who are at present moving in this general direction of untraveled paths of the dance.

The principles of these studies are applicable to any and all religious convictions, whether Roman Catholic or Quaker, Buddhist or Sufi, whether of Taoist or Islam, for basically they never change.

Among the most valuable works on this whole subject is Ted Shawn's *Every Little Movement*, which is a book about François Delsarte and his discoveries on the subject of the relationship between thought and motion and the "zones" of the human body. What Delsarte revealed, I still consider after many years of research, indestructible and universal in its application to the art of dance and drama.

Appendices

APPENDIX A

Selections from "An Unfinished Life"

Miss Ruth's autobiography, *An Unfinished Life* (1939), describes various influences on her life. True to form, she mixes in the past and the present, ideas and events. I have not changed this, but will give a bit of background to provide a context for her comments.

Miss Ruth's mother was a Methodist and read the Bible often to her. From an early age, Ruthie was her confidant. Ruth's mother used the Bible as her aid in a difficult relationship with Ruth's father, a man who was a dreamer and never really provided for his family. When Ruth was about eleven, she read the New Testament on her own. Being a highly creative, imaginative and sensitive child, she took the story of the Passion in a very deep way. She became so identified with Jesus, she took boards, towels and sandals to an unused room in the large farm house. Here she reinacted the Passion.

> For that moment I believed myself the little Jesus, and a curious flame burned in me that, in the light of later wisdom, can only be interpreted as a faint but intense identification with cosmic

consciousness. When the mood passed, and I took off my robe and sandals, and went downstairs again to take up the normal living, I had touched a divine spark that was later to burn in me with increasing intensity. (p. 7)

By contrast, she experienced worship in church as dull and formal, with depressing hymns and morbid sermons, nothing like her living experience of the divine.

As she became a teenager and the family moved from the New Jersey farm into New York City, her mother believed Ruth needed more education. She was sent to Packer Collegiate Institute where she had her next awakening to Christianity.

> The Packer Collegiate Institute meant neither more or less to me than any other place of confinement until I took part, one day, in a service in the Gothic chapel. The enormous impression it made on me is not surprising. Until now I had only experienced the comforting but drab little service of Mother's church. Here instead was an organ, a choir singing all the solemn hymns of the Episcopal Service. Its impact was so unexpected and dynamic I might very easily have been drawn toward the extreme. (p.26)

Of course Mother was ever present to bring Ruthie back to earth. By now she had become an actress and was touring with David Belasco's troupe in *Madame Dubarry*. It was summer and touring was halted for a rest. Ruth's mother and father were away, and she was in her own small apartment in Manhattan with her brother Buzz. Lying on the couch one Sunday afternoon while wondering where she was going and what she was doing, she found the key to the mystery.

> It had lain on the shelf above my head for a long time but was not discovered till this Sunday afternoon when I reached out an arm to pick up the only book in our small library I had not read. It proved

to be a brown-covered book called *Science and Health, with Key to the Scriptures,* by Mary Baker Eddy....

What happened to my consciousness might have indeed have been achieved by any other scriptures of the world, but the fact remains that it was this particular book which revealed a new dimension to my thought and feeling. (p. 46)

To ponder the ideas in this book she went on long walks in New York City.

My strolls were empty of any outward incident but filled me with wonder and a strange inward vibration which was unlike anything I had ever known before.

This definite condition of spiritual ecstasy remained with me for some weeks and then gradually faded, and left as a residue a love of spiritual things and a realization of metaphysical values which has been with me always. (pp. 46-47)

Working for David Belasco as an actress, Miss Ruth toured many states and even spent time in England. She did bit parts and occasionally danced in plays. Because of her purity David Belasco called her "St. Denis," and so Ruthie Dennis became, as she used to say, canonized. While touring in Buffalo, New York, she and her best friend went out for an ice cream soda. Sitting in the ice cream parlor, Miss Ruth glanced up at the wall opposite her and fell into a trance: here was a poster of Isis sitting on a throne, an ad for a cigarette brand. After they left she begged her friend to return and buy the poster for her. Miss Ruth had discovered her true purpose.

She began working on her first original dance production, *Radha, Delirium of the Senses.* To prepare for this, Miss Ruth immersed herself in the teachings of the Orient. She researched costuming and looked for native Indians to help her get the right atmosphere for her dance. Finally, in January 1906 in New York's Hudson Theater, *Radha* was performed.

It must be remembered that my creative instincts were, and at the same were not, those of a dancer.... Without any question I was at that time a kind of dancing ritualist. The intensities of my spiritual life had found a focus of action in exactly the same way that another earnest young person would enter the church. I longed to translate into rhythmic patterns spiritual significance. This had not been done, so far as I know, in the Western world.... For there is a vast and psychological difference between a dancer, moving on the altar before an image of a god in propitiation or sacrifice or praise, and the embodiment by the dancer of the elements which he [sic] conceives to belong to the godhead. (p. 57)

She next developed the second part of her trinity, the art of the dance. Finally doing what she loved, she discovered she was not immune to pain and sorrow.

Though I have remained devoted, with a daily and constant fidelity, to the Bible and all of its development in modern thought, I became at once a citizen of another realm when I first began my research into the vast wisdom of the East. And yet even with my expanding concept of life I did not escape periods of horrible depression when the delightful and awful phantasmagoria of my career was living out its hectic hours. Where, for instance, was I, the immortal essential Me, when the Ruthie Dennis, canonized by David Belasco into an undeserved sainthood, was dancing her way around the world?

One's whole career, in retrospect, seems only a great first act to an uncompleted drama of the soul. (p. 74)

She went on tour to England in July 1906 and there made connections with other artists and an impresario who took charge of her career in Europe. Of her time in Paris she wrote

During all these days of excitement and adulation I never forgot that in these performances I was doing something besides entertaining the public. The spiritual levels of my life flowed ever underneath, and supported and gave direction to all that appeared on the surface. Mother's faith in the goodness of God, my own realizations, derived from Christian Science, were holding even in these confusions, unpleasant though they were. At this time I began a

custom which lasted 5-6 years of dancing Radha. My approach
to the performance... was at least a half hour of meditation....
By the time I had left to go on stage I was truly a priestess in the
temple. (pp. 86-87)

She went on to greater fame in Germany, and all over the European continent.

At this time, however, my religious impulses were uncompromisingly
metaphysical. It is true that two elements in my nature would seem
to deny the validity of this cold dispassion—the dancing of an
Oriental ritual and my brief forays into romantic love. From one
viewpoint they were irreconcilable, from another I was merely an
intellectual religionist; but it took me many years to learn this fact,
and in the meanwhile the three possessors of my nature were in
constant conflict. From the moral and theoretical point of view I
knew all the answers, but my proud, willful, pleasure-seeking heart
would never surrender itself to the discipline of spiritual teachings.
My life was, unconsciously, departmentalized in both its motives
and its demonstrations. My capacity for love had never been
expressed in all its dynamic fullness. My art life had been kept
separate from my spiritual life except for brief moments of
illumination when I sensed how they supplement each other. And to
make my life of spirit and mind and heart even more difficult, each
element was as real and pressing as the other. (pp. 105-106)

Returning to the United States in November 1909 and on her first tour
there she reflected

Every time I danced before an audience I wished to say through my
body that man [sic], in all his arts and spiritual perception, must be
worshipping the godhead whatever name it is called, Jehovah,
Brahma, Allah. The few who perceived this only made me reach the
farther to touch all those who came for entertainment and went
away merely entertained. (p. 136)

As her second tour progressed she came to realize

I have been shocked and alarmed when I realized all too clearly that
I was producing these religious dances in the theaters of the world

Wisdom comes dancing...

and getting paid for it. But as I said before, I had not then made a complete design of this new form of religious expression. I had gotten only so far as the personal expression, but it really had not occurred to me to try and battle my way to build a theater temple in which not only my own conceptions but others of similar inspiration could be adequately produced and protected. At this time, Isadora and I, and others who had forsworn the orthodoxies of ballet, were busy waging our war to make America accept dancing as an art. To compel it to accept the dance as an instrument of worship was something still to come. (p. 140)

Then in 1914, the third god in her trinity demanded to be noticed.

I had paid constant service to the other gods of my idolatry. I had brought my adorations to the feet of Beauty and Wisdom, but now my god of Love, so long neglected, was commanding my presence in his sanctuary on pain of death of all progress and all joy. For does not Wisdom spring from Love, and is not Beauty the very form of Desire?

Fragments of the old assurances came to my mind as I sat there. 'Before thou speakest, I will answer...'.

Within ten days Ted Shawn stood in this same room. (p. 155)

They danced together and created a school called Denishawn that trained many of the famous dancers to come, such as Martha Graham, Doris Humphrey and Charles Weidman. They also were married. Miss Ruth, a creative genius, admitted fully to having no organizational skills. A school with routines and schedules was not really suited to her temperament. Ted, too, had his own ideas and the two very strong egos often clashed. As she said, they did not complement each other in combusting the fires that lead to unleashed creativity; both had the need and desire to be individually creative.

A deeper question even than our artistic dissonances was the perpetual fact that my three gods could not dwell together. I must make my obeisances to one god at a time; otherwise they destroyed me. Each god jealously demanded my entire obedience, affection, and strength.

Art, religion, and love: what a glorious and divergent trinity! In the unseen these are one, and their name is realization of life, the perfect kingdom within—Nirvana. But in time and space they are seemingly irreconcilable. (p. 209)

Nature had been a strong, abiding source of comfort and inspiration to Miss Ruth from childhood. It gave her a key to her next step.

It has always been my instinct to relate the dance to nature. I can not remember a time when the rhythms of nature have not controlled my whole being. I have always felt an intuitive wish to identify my body with the long sway of the sea as it falls against the shore, or the subtle movement of the pines when they move in an evening breeze.... In motions of animals, too, I find a curious kinship; and the elements—wind, rain, sea, fire—and the long hotness of the desert have all been translated into my articulation. (p. 220)

Longing to create once again the dances that were part of her very soul, she conceived the ballet *Ishtar of the Seven Gates* in 1922.

For a long time I had been grieving that I had been unable to produce these semi-mystical, semi-religious dances that I felt were my special talent. For years now I had been upon a rack which pulled from the left my human side and on the right all I might become. What the public saw in *Ishtar* was a momentary manifestation of that rare state when for a few precious hours my spiritual and physical equilibrium was attained.

To me there is only one real drama: the drama of humanity's struggle to emerge from the limitation imposed by our own concept of time and space. The symbol of *Egypta* [another of Miss Ruth's dances] was the balanced faculties of the bisexual or complete being, expressed in the negative and positive of day and night, in the manifold culture of woman and man, and in the complete cycle of life and death. *Radha* was the symbol of realization, that comes only by a complete denial of the attachments of sense does one experience the golden lotus of illumination. *Ishtar* was the desire principle of creation, that living power that manifested itself first in human love and passion and then in the ramifications of those energies of love which are expressed in the combativeness of war, in the imagery of the arts and in the illumination of religion.

In the future I hope to produce a fourth conception: Mary, the Madonna. Mary was to symbolize the ultimate creating principle which embraces compassion as well as creation.

My final use to art is impersonal, for when I dance I am really an abstraction, a creature set apart by time and space, unrelated to human things in the ordinary sense. I feel a certain limitless state of being, a curious unending movement not only of my dance, but of my being. I could go on without cessation, subject only to the necessary limits of the body. (pp. 241-242)

Miss Ruth's relationship with Ted Shawn produced various schools of dance. The first school was in Los Angeles. Later they started schools in New York, with branches all over the country. She saw the goal of these schools going beyond mere technique.

We held steadfastly to our belief that Denishawn should be more than an institution, that it should be a philosophy. We wanted to give students not a rigid technique, but rather such a power that whatever their professional life demanded they would be able to respond with perfect assurance. To those who were planning no career, and even those who were, we wanted to give an intimate understanding of the arts, so that this wide culture would be as familiar to them as the steps they learned....

We wanted the school to be a stream for ideas, and I think we succeeded, although Ted and I were aware we bore a prince and were raising it like a stepchild. (pp. 243-244)

In this connection, she mentioned the books that helped her get through the constant touring. (See Appendix B for the list.) She also talked about the purposes of her own writing.

> The writing of my journals served a double purpose: one was the
> release of my emotional feelings, and the record of the currents set
> in motion by books and objective happenings; the other was a subtle
> and very powerful liberation that came when, in great distress and
> fear, I wrote out my prayers and affirmations. (p. 248)

Although at the height of the Denishawn popularity the money was good,
Miss Ruth's expenses were just as great. To establish the kind of school they
envisioned, with its own building and land, was an expensive proposition.
Both Ted and Miss Ruth had a terrible fear of debt. Even though they hated to
do vaudeville it was the only way they knew to make the money they needed.
It was particularly discouraging when they discovered that foreign dancers
received greater institutional support in the U.S. than they did.

> I had quite a struggle over the Russian ballet. In the midst of one of
> our busiest seasons, when as a native American art we were making
> an effort to keep our foothold, we learned that the ballet had a
> guarantee from the Metropolitan Opera management that their
> debts up to a startling degree would be absorbed. (p. 256)

In 1925 at the end of one of the Denishawn tours, their manager, Daniel
Mayer, announced that he had made a contract for them to tour the Far East.
After all the talk and imaginings of the Orient, here was an opportunity for
all to experience it first hand. Miss Ruth spoke of her ambivalent feelings.

> How can I describe my feelings? Part of me responded with the
> same spontaneous joy as the others, but the deeper, more intimate
> part of me was depressed beyond words. When I went to the Orient
> I wanted to go alone; I did not want to take the endless jangling of
> company and performances and drudgery that had infected the last
> twelve years. I wanted to bring a sensitive, alive instrument to
> absorb not only the aesthetic wonders of the ancient East, but those
> deeper realizations of the universal human spirit in its quest for
> reality. (pp. 257-258)

They had nine months to prepare for their tour to the Orient. It was a busy and hectic time. Miss Ruth described her journey and the tour with excerpts from her journals. They met with tremendous acclaim everywhere. It is astonishing how many places they did go, all by ship. Here is a quote from the *Japan Advertiser*:

> "It is natural for the Japanese to look to America and conclude nothing new can be found in the land of radio and automobiles. But an evening at the Imperial Theater was enough to revolutionize our opinion.
>
> The Denishawn Dancers convinced Japanese that America is now creating its own art, moreover it has something very suggestive of the future. Whenever an historian tries to write a book on the relations between Japan and United States, he cannot ignore the coming of the Denishawn Dancers in 1925 to Japan, because with their appearance on the stage of Tokyo, the attitude toward America in respect to art is completely changed." (p. 267)

On October 2, 1925 Miss Ruth unknowingly saw into her own future. She described her meeting with a retiring geisha.

> Kyoto, Theater of the Geisha: We greet an extraordinary old lady, Mme. Katayama, who is retiring from active stage work, on her eighty-eighth birthday!
>
> There she sits—eighty-eight years old and still dancing. She moves now with tremendous power. (p. 273)

Miss Ruth discovered that she had as much to give as to receive from all the wonderful places they visited. She discovered that her deep connection to the East and its spiritual teachings was on the inside and had not so much to do with the outer circumstances.

Two years later the company returned to the United States and felt it must give an account of the time spent in the Orient to the audiences here. Miss

Ruth became discouraged with criticism that they were watering down their dances for the general public.

> I was in revolt. It seemed to me that for years Ted and I had drudged and endured, and now I wanted some harmony between my inner and outer lives. I suppose another artist would have been satisfied with the success that had come to me. Why was I, then, so restless and unsatisfied?
>
> Because I knew my essential offering was creative and not interpretive, and for me to go on week after week and year after year repeating my used up creations, while my whole being cried for new forms, brought me only despair. It was inevitable that in order to express any part of the purely spiritual dances which were my soul as an artist I must show them in distorted form, in an alien environment. (p. 306)

Together with Miss Ruth and Ted Shawn, everyone who worked with the company had a dream they called the Greater Denishawn. This was a wide range of places and activities that would fulfill their vision of the arts.

> This dream was to include not only country acreage and a colony, a theater for the American dance, a magazine, but a hundred new branches of education and knowledge of the dance and its cooperating arts which reached beyond anything we were able to achieve heretofore. I was to have my temple for my religious ideas of the dance, and eventually a chapel to demonstrate them in....
>
> It was evident that this plan naturally could come into expression only by the cooperation of us all, and here is where our heartburnings, our weakness, and our egotisms came to grief.... We could easily go ahead with our plans of a physical structure of Denishawn House, but something deeper was needed to make it a logical step toward the greater things we planned. As I look back now, I see those adjustments were never made. (pp. 307-308)

Ted left the tour briefly and bought property in Van Cortlandt Park in New York City. Meanwhile the tour was rapidly heading toward Manhattan for the

Wisdom comes dancing...

triumphant return of the Denishawn Dancers from the Orient. Three hundred people were turned away from their New York City performance. In the thrill of the success, amidst the cheers, Miss Ruth commited an enormous faux pas. She went on stage alone and talked about the plan for the Greater Denishawn, giving the impression the idea was hers alone.

> There was great applause and apparently a warm response to my words. But when I stepped backstage I realized I had made an unpardonable mistake. Ted was furious. As far as he was concerned I had negated him and all his years of devotion, all his plans and his identification with Denishawn. I had presented myself in the guise of the solitary head of the whole organization.

> June sided with him, and I could make no amends now that the damage was done.... The years that we spent working together in such close harness necessarily caused certain faculties and attributes of our separate beings to lie undeveloped or atrophied. And, both consciously and unconsciously, we were seeking to assert our full and individual stature. But the reverberations of that speech echoed in our lives until the end of Denishawn. (p. 309)

Meanwhile, in spite of the great mistake, plans went on for building the Denishawn house in Van Cortlandt Park. The house was also meant to be a private home and studio for Miss Ruth and Ted. Money was needed for this building as well as for the Greater Denishawn, so Ted and Ruth signed with a version of the Ziegfeld Follies to go on tour again. When she saw the completed building, Miss Ruth said, "Every brick a one-night stand."

During a Christmas break of four days they rushed back to the completed house, joyous to finally have a studio and home. But Miss Ruth commented

> The next morning we stood again on the roof, and then our serpent entered this Eden. Country people speak of land lust. I had never understood it before. But now we looked over the parapet on the eastside and saw four lots which in our imagination were already occupied by someone else and depriving us of light. We looked

north and saw a house which had been started. At once we decided to buy the lots and the house—oh, irony—to protect ourselves. (p. 311)

Many people lived and danced at Denishawn house including Doris Humphrey and Charles Weidman. For seven years it functioned as an artistic and spiritual center, but Miss Ruth also called it "this house that started to be a home and ended as a tomb of buried loves and plans" (p. 312).

Many important people of the day came to the Denishawn House. Here is where Miss Ruth delivered many of the talks included in this book and where she worked on the manuscript of "The Divine Dance." Overwhelming debts forced the 1934 demise of Denishawn House and the end of the Greater Denishawn plan. Ted had already started to make plans for Jacob's Pillow, his own center for dance in Massachusetts. In 1931 Miss Ruth and he danced together one more time at Lewisohn Stadium in New York.

The selling of the house, the dissolution of her relationship with Ted, both personal and professional, along with the new wave of modern dance especially from Germany, took Miss Ruth on a downward spiral, questioning her own self-worth.

> In these last years at Denishawn House I felt like someone marooned on a desert island, without help in sight. In this spiritually empty house I was fighting sometimes jealously, sometimes despairingly, to retain something of my own confidence in the value and power of my destiny. (p. 331)

She moved to a loft space that a friend converted for her. Ruth Harwood, a friend and artist who illustrated the *Lotus Light* poems, encouraged Miss Ruth to start her Society for Spiritual Arts again. Without fully knowing it, Miss Ruth embarked on her next career. People came from all spiritual backgrounds—Swami Nikliananda, Manly P. Hall, and Dr. Sum Nung au-Young, a translator of the Tao Te Ching. Miss Ruth was also invited by several churches to give a ritual of the Masque of Mary as part of the worship service. About this performance, she commented

> Here, perhaps for the first time in a Christian temple, was my initial gesture toward the production of a Christian temple dance. I had a consciousness that the audience understood the symbolism of the pageant....
>
> This was all very satisfying, but I began to feel, aside from the expense involved in these productions, that they were going wide of the basic intention of the temple. (pp. 365-366)

Ever the seeker and never satisfied with easy success, Miss Ruth felt she must probe the deeper, unsolved emotional questions that plagued her and the people around her.

> Before I speak of this next period of my life, I want to state in utmost simplicity that I have always tried to relate the outward actions of my emotional life to an inner ideal. It has been this spiritual necessity which has caused my subjective sufferings all these years. Had I accepted lesser planes of activity, mere self indulgences and the compromises that go with a supposedly Bohemian existence, I would not have suffered. (p. 367)

Miss Ruth discovered love—a true, deep love that was as satisfying to the body as to the soul. She felt a deep and holy connection with an oriental man she described as a poet and philosopher. He asked nothing of her and only wanted to share what they had together, with no demands or expectations. This was so new and profound an experience that after a time Miss Ruth was overwhelmed and ran away. Finally, she ran all the way to England. Here she discovered the Oxford Group, a Christian pacifist organization which was the precursor of the Movement for Moral Re-Armament.

Upon her return, Paul Eddy, President of Adelphi College and a former attendee of Miss Ruth's temple meetings, met her again.

> He asked me to create a dance department, where the technical and artistic phases of the modern and Oriental would be balanced by certain manifestations of the temple, which he felt made a definite contribution to the integration of religion and the arts. (p. 385)

Of course, Miss Ruth did not stop here, but her unfinished life in this book form did.

APPENDIX B

Bibliography of Miss Ruth's 'Constant Companions' from Lists in "An Unfinished Life"

Books by Evelyn Underhill on mysticism

Ralph Waldo Emerson

The Bhagavad Gita

The Bible

Buddha and the Gospel of Buddhism, Dr. Ananda Coomaraswami

Little Essays of Love and Virtue, Havelock Ellis

Christ and the Indian Road, Stanley Jones

The Travel Diary of a Philosopher, Count Keyserling

The Gate Beautiful, Stimpson

The Gleam, Sir Francis Youngblood

God is My Adventure, Rom Landau

Science and Health, Mary Baker Eddy

The Practice of the Presence of God, Brother Lawrence

The Light of Asia, Sir Edwin Arnold

Tertium Organum, P. D. Ouspensky

Bibliography

Graham, Martha. *Blood Memory.* New York: Harper Collins, 1991.

Humphrey, Doris. *The Art of Making Dances.* New York, Grove Press, 1959.

Humphrey, Doris. "New Dance: An Unfinished Autobiography." *Dance Perspectives,* 1966.

Rogosin, Elinor, ed. *The Dance Makers: Conversations with American Choreographers.* New York: Walker & Co., 1980.

Shawn, Ted. *Ruth St. Denis, Pioneer and Prophet.* San Francisco: J.H. Nash, 1920.

Shelton, Suzanne. *Divine Dancer: A Biography of Ruth St. Denis.* Garden City, NY: Doubleday, 1981.

Schlundt, Christina. *The Professional Appearances of Ruth St. Denis and Ted Shawn, A Chronology and an Index of Dances from 1906-1932.* New York: New York Public Library, 1962.

St. Denis, Ruth. *Lotus Light.* New York: Houghton and Mifflin, 1932.

St. Denis, Ruth. "The Divine Dance." Unpublished manuscript, 1934.

St. Denis, Ruth. *An Unfinished Life. Dance Horizons* reprint of New York & London: Harper and Brothers, 1939.

St. Denis, Ruth. Unpublished manuscripts from University of California at Los Angeles, Ruth St. Denis collection, various dates.

Terry, Walter. *Dance In America.* New York: Harper and Row, 1956.

Terry, Walter. *Miss Ruth, The "More Living Life" of Ruth St. Denis.* New York: Dodd, Mead and Co., 1969.

Resources

» **PeaceWorks International Network for the Dances of Universal Peace** provides information on various activities throughout the world on the Dances of Universal Peace, as well as books, cassettes, and resources for peace through the arts. For information about memberships, publications, or dance events around the world, contact

> PeaceWorks
> PeaceWorks Publications
> International Network for the
> Dances of Universal Peace
> PO Box 55994
> Seattle, WA 98155-0994 USA
> 206-522-4353
> peaceworkspubs@dancesofuniversalpeace.org

» **The Ruth St. Denis Foundation** is an organization for the preservation of the dances of Ruth St. Denis. For a schedule of activities and other information, contact

> Karoun Tootikian, Director
> Ruth St. Denis Foundation
> 618 S. Sycamore Avenue
> Los Angeles, CA 90036
> USA
> 213.934.8643

About the Editor

Kamae A Miller, MA (Creativity and Spirituality), is a writer, artist, and teacher of sacred movement in the Sufi tradition. For the past ten years she has facilitated workshops on women's spirituality, dance, walking meditation, and creativity in the U.S., Canada, Europe, Russia, and Australia. She currently lives in England.